# The Ultimate
# Japanese Phrasebook

S0-AUZ-403

# The Ultimate Japanese Phrasebook

## 1800 Sentences for Everyday Use

### Kit Pancoast Nagamura
### Kyoko Tsuchiya

Narrated by
Reiko Matsunaga and Tatsuhiro Nishinosono
with Katie Adler and Jeff Gedert

Illustrated by
Shinsaku Sumi

KODANSHA INTERNATIONAL
Tokyo • New York • London

Parental advisory: This book and the accompanying CD contain language that may be unsuitable for young readers. Parental discretion is advised.

Japanese narration by arrangement with PSC Produce and Management. CD recording and editing by The English Language Education Council Inc.

Distributed in the United States by Kodansha America, LLC, and in the United Kingdom and continental Europe by Kodansha Europe Ltd.

Published by Kodansha International Ltd., 17-14 Otowa 1-chome, Bunkyo-ku, Tokyo 112-8652.

First edition, 2009
18 17 16 15 14 13 12 11 10 09      10 9 8 7 6 5 4 3 2 1


Library of Congress Cataloging-in-Publication Data

Nagamura, Kit Pancoast.
    The ultimate Japanese phrasebook : 1800 sentences for everyday use / Kit Pancoast Nagamura, Kyoko Tsuchiya ; narrated by Reiko Matsunaga and Tatsuhiro Nishinosono ; illustrated by Shinsaku Sumi. — 1st ed.
        p. cm.
    Issued with 1 MP3 audio CD.
    ISBN 978-4-7700-3100-6
1.   Japanese language—Conversation and phrase books—English.   I. Tsuchiya, Kyoko. II. Title.
    PL539.N24 2009
    495.6'5—dc22
                        2009026345

**www.kodansha-intl.com**

# CONTENTS

Preface    14
A Note on the Translations    16
How to Listen to the Audio    18
Complete Newbie Briefer    20

## CHAPTER 1 **The Basics**                              22

Essentials    22
Meeting and Greeting    24
Introducing Yourself    26
Introducing Others    27
Exit Lines    29
What? Where?    30
When? Who?    32
Why? How?    33
Can and Need    35
Food, Water, and Shelter    36

## CHAPTER 2 **Me, Myself, and I**                        38

Family    38
Children    39
Education    40
Hobbies and Interests    42

Work    43

Personal History    44

Likes and Dislikes    46

Personality    47

Values    48

Goals and Aspirations    50

## CHAPTER 3   **A Time and a Place**    52

By the Clock    52

Yesterday, Today, and Tomorrow    53

Week In and Week Out    55

Months and Years    56

Next Month, Last Year    57

Periodically Speaking    59

Sooner or Later    60

Timely Remarks    61

The Time of Your Life    62

A Matter of Timing    63

## CHAPTER 4   **Shopping**    65

Drugstore Items    65

Groceries    66

Furniture    68

Clothing Styles    69

Clothing Sizes and Materials    70

Electronics    72

Appliances    73

Beauty Products    75

Art and Antiques    76

Gifts and Traditional Items    78

Payment    79

## CHAPTER 5 **Getting Around** 81

Getting Directions    81

Giving Directions    82

Train and Subway    84

Buses and Taxis    85

Cars and Roads    87

Bicycles and Motorcycles    88

Airplanes and Airports    90

Boats and Ferries    91

On Foot    92

## CHAPTER 6 **Eating Out** 94

Scoping Out the Place    94

Ordering    95

Questions    96

Concerns and Requests    98

Complaints    99

Compliments    100

Settling the Bill    102

Unique Situations    103

## CHAPTER 7 **Hanging with Friends** 105

Invitations    105

Details    107

When the Party Starts    108

Table Talk    109

Ordering Delivery    110

How's the Food?    111

Lay It Out on the Table    112

Parting and Postmortem    114

## CHAPTER 8  Talking about People    117

Physique    117

Hair    119

Ears, Eyes, Nose, and Lips    120

Limbs    122

Chest, Belly, and Buns    123

Overall Looks    124

Personality: Good Traits    125

Personality: Bad Traits    128

Lifestyle    131

## CHAPTER 9  Social Interaction    133

Initiating a Chat    133

Getting and Giving Opinions    134

Agreeing and Disagreeing    135

Making Suggestions    137

Hesitating and Resisting    138

Words of Encouragement    139

Getting Things Straight    141

Equivocating, Deliberating, and Stonewalling    143

Taking and Relinquishing Control    144

Cooling and Consoling    146

Compliments    147

Criticisms    149

Insults and Incendiaries    150

Apologies and Excuses    151

Forgiving and Forgetting    152

## CHAPTER 10 **Feelings** 154

Happiness    154

Sadness    155

Confidence and Determination    156

Gratitude    157

Anxiety    158

Sympathy    159

Self-pity and Regret    161

Irritation    162

Hope and Excitement    164

Wonder and Curiosity    165

Indignation    166

Confusion and Doubt    167

Indifference    168

Shock and Awe    170

Weariness and Wellness    171

Depression and Trauma    172

## CHAPTER 11 **On the Job** 175

Initial Reconnaissance    175

Setting Up an Interview    176

The Interview    178

Comments, Questions, and Self-assessments    179

On the Job    181

To and From the Office    182

Telephone Calls    183

Meetings, Memos, Functions, and E-mail    185

Contracts, Salaries, Wages, and Benefits    186

Working Well or Working Hell    188

## CHAPTER 12  Home Sweet Home                           190

Apartment Hunting    190

The Walk-through    191

Follow-up Questions    193

Checking and Signing    194

Electricity, Gas, and Water    197

Repairs and Complaints    198

Services and Facilities    199

Logistic Details    201

Moving In    202

## CHAPTER 13  Getting Stuff Done                         205

At Home    205

At the Bank    206

At the Post Office    209

By Courier    210

Getting Phones and Phone Lines    211

Accessing Internet and E-mail    213

Making Business Cards    214

Getting Repairs    215

Media Access    217

Dealing with Documents    218

## CHAPTER 14  Health and Beauty    221

Doctor's Office    221

Medications    222

Conditions and Symptoms    224

Dentist, Orthodontist, Optometrist    225

Exercise    227

Barber and Salon    229

Esthetic Treatments and Cosmetic Surgery    231

Self-assessment    233

Diet and Reactions to Food    234

Special Circumstances    236

## CHAPTER 15  The Private Zone    238

Getting Started or Stalled    238

Sweet Talk    240

Going Out    242

Moving Forward    243

Getting Into It    245

Climax and Pillow Talk    246

Commitment    248

Clarifications and Complications    250

Anger and Apology    253

Kiss 'n' Tell    255

## CHAPTER 16 **Babies, Kids, and Teens** 257

Baby Conceptions   257

Babies on the Loose   258

Playground Debut   260

Nursery School   261

Kindergarten   263

Elementary School   265

Middle School and High School   266

University   268

Alternative Education   269

Talking to Other People's Kids   270


## CHAPTER 17 **Troubleshooting and Emergencies** 273

Calls for Help   273

Ambulance   274

Hospital   276

Fire and Police   277

Traffic Accidents and Incidents   278

Fight and Flight   280

Dangers   282

Train Situations   283

Panic at the Disco   284


## CHAPTER 18 **Special Events** 287

Births, Birthdays, and Anniversaries   287

Engagements and Weddings   288

School Events   290

Company Events    291

Personal Events and Milestones    292

Holiday Events    294

Funerals    295

Stressful Challenges    297

Achievements    298

## CHAPTER **19**  **Just for Fun**

300

Cultural Explorations    300

Pets    301

Sports    302

Rural Adventure    303

Cooking    305

Ryokans and Hot Springs    306

Museums and Galleries    308

Sightseeing and Photography    309

Concerts and Movies    311

Road Trips    312

Lazing About    313

Reading and Watching TV    314

Language Study    316

Acknowledgments    318

# PREFACE

*The Ultimate Japanese Phrasebook* might seem like a grandiose title. It *is* a bit out there, but my coauthor and I believe that this book will prove the ultimate boon to anyone with an interest in speaking Japanese. The phrases included are specifically designed to help English speakers who plan to stay in Japan—expats, business visitors, English teachers, exchange students, cross-cultural newlyweds—say exactly what they want to say in colloquial Japanese. There are many phrasebooks aimed at Japanese learners of conversational English, but this is the first to reverse the point of view. The book is also useful for tourists who want to make connections during travel in Japan, students of Japanese seeking a pinch of lingo to make their Nihongo go, armchair travelers, and even Japanese eager for insight into native-English phraseology.

Inside the compact format of *The Ultimate Japanese Phrasebook*, you'll find nineteen chapters of pithy, crucial, useful expressions divided into subcategories ranging from the basics of "Meeting and Greeting" all the way to the likes of "On the Job," "Kiss 'n' Tell," and even "Fight and Flight." The first ten chapters cover what you'd need to know to make friends and connections in Japanese, and the final nine are more detailed and geared toward setting up a life in Japan.

All 1800 phrases in this book appear in their natural Japanese form (with furigana over the kanji characters) and in romanized Japanese for reading ease. Additionally, each phrase has been recorded in English and in Japanese on the MP3 CD at the back. Both male and female professional narrators were chosen to demonstrate the intended intonation and implied nuance of each phrase, as well as the subtle distinctions between Japanese male and female language (though it is interesting to note such distinctions have begun to blur). Simply download the MP3 files to your laptop, phone, or music player, and you've got your Japanese lessons on the go. We've even kept the book as light and compact as possible, because the more places it goes with you, the happier we are.

What's unique about this phrasebook is that it keeps things real; the expressions are in their most natural, colloquial form. If we found a phrase in English that could not be rendered comfortably in conversational Japanese, we dumped it. We've gone out on a limb to include as many aspects of real life as possible, including pets and parties, shopping and sex, shouts of joy, and even curses (parental discretion is advised) to bring a compendium that cannot be found in any dictionary or language textbook to date.

Here's one phrase that might shock you: Japanese is not a terribly difficult language to speak. Next to German, French, or Chinese, spoken Japanese is a walk in the park in terms of pronunciation and structure, and the verb forms used in daily conversation have a mere handful of variations to grasp. We'd like to emphasize this: everyday Japanese has an everyday brevity and casual feel to it that is easy to grok, once you have a guide.

Kyoko and I, and our talented editor, Michael Staley, are all seasoned bilingual residents of Japan who are committed to sharing the fun of communicating across cultures. We have created the kind of book we really wished we had had back when we were first learning each other's language. We feel this book makes the vivid, impulsive, energetic world of English language come alive in matching Japanese. We had a great time, learning and laughing as we tried out each other's languages. We hope you will too!

Kit Pancoast Nagamura

# A NOTE ON THE TRANSLATIONS

Spoken language is a life form, and as such it changes and evolves. Not only that, but the meaning of a conversation can often be taken only in context, every element of a situation adding a layer of meaning: the speaker's personality and status, what is happening at the moment, or any other of countless factors.

With this in mind, the reader will understand that the Japanese translations of the phrases in this book are by no means the only correct ones, nor are they applicable or advisable for use in every situation. Be sure to read and consider the subheadings in each chapter to get an idea of the sort of conversation in which each phrase would be useful.

Our first priority for *The Ultimate Japanese Phrasebook* was to introduce expressions that would make for lively and natural spoken Japanese. While relentlessly sticking to this point, we kept the phrases short enough for beginners to learn. Some, therefore, ignore the rules of grammar and others have bold omissions—but isn't that what conversation is all about? Just make sure you don't use the phrases as samples for written expression!

As we all know, punctuation is meant to clarify the meaning of a sentence and give it rhythm. In this book, however, we have used punctuation more as an aide for the beginning Japanese reader than as a model for written Japanese. We have added commas to break up strings of words in hiragana that would otherwise be nexttoimpossibletoseparate and make sense of.

Students of Japanese quickly learn that a major difficulty in the language is "words for men" and "words for women." The more casual the conversation, the greater the problem. To avoid it, we have done our best to make *The Ultimate Japanese Phrasebook* as gender-neutral as possible. Please note, though, that such an attempt softens male language a tad, and adds a hint of masculinity to female language. In cases where it has been impossible to use a single phrase for both genders, "M" indicates the male version, and "F" the female.

All in all, we are pleased and satisfied with what we have achieved here, given the space constraints, and we think you will be, too. *The Ultimate Japanese Phrase-*

*book* will stand you in good stead when you want to make yourself clear or need to get something off your chest and get on with life. Each and every phrase in the book is a natural and appealing form of expression. Stick to it and you'll soon have more friends to speak Japanese with. Here's to your success!

Kyoko Tsuchiya

# HOW TO LISTEN TO THE AUDIO

The MP3 CD that comes with this book is for use with computers, MP3 players, and CD players that can play MP3 audio files. Standard CD players without MP3 compatibility will not be able to play it.

The audio was designed with users of iTunes in mind, but the MP3 files can also be played on other media players, such as QuickTime or Windows Media Player.

To listen to the audio in iTunes:

1. Insert the CD into your computer.
2. Double-click on the CD icon to open it.
3. Select all the files by pressing Apple-A or Command-A (on a Mac), or Control-A (on any other type of PC).
4. Drag and drop the files into iTunes, either by dropping them on the iTunes application icon or by opening iTunes and dragging the files into the music library window. Be sure that "Copy files to iTunes Music folder when adding to library," under "Advanced" in iTunes "Preferences" (in the iTunes menu bar), is checked.

To download the files to your iPod or other MP3 player after you have performed the above steps, just plug the device into your computer and sync it.

# The Ultimate
# Japanese Phrasebook

# Complete Newbie Briefer

*If you are utterly new to Japanese, these two pages will give you a whirlwind intro to some key elements of the language.*

## Pronunciation

*Vowels.* Long or short, the sound of vowels is consistent. If long, simply give it a stronger emphasis, and you're fine.

| | |
|---|---|
| **a** as in Ah! | Example: **akachan** (baby) |
| **e** as in Hey! | Example: **ē to . . .** (Let me see . . .) |
| **i** as in Eek! | Example: **itadakimasu** (Let's eat) |
| **o** as in Oh my! | Example: **Osoi yo!** (You're late!) |
| **u** as in Moo! | Example: **Urusai ne!** (What a lot of noise!) |

In this book we use macrons to show long vowels: ā, ē, ī, ō, ū.

*Consonants.* Most consonants in Japanese follow the hard sound in English (**g** as in great, **b** as in boring, **k** as in crazy, etc.), but there are two exceptions: (1) **f** is as in fool, but breathy, like "who" with an "f" sound, and (2) **r**, which hides between an "l" and "r" sound. Place your tongue in the middle of your mouth when you say "r," don't let it touch your teeth or the roof of your mouth, and you'll come close to pronouncing the Japanese **r**.

When the same consonant appears one after the other in the middle of a word—like in **matte** (wait)—pause for the first consonant, much as you would when you say "not today," skipping over the first "t" but clearly voicing the second.

## Word Order

Unlike the subject-verb-object sentence organization of English, Japanese sentences tend to follow a subject-object-verb transition (which in translation sounds a little bit like the grammar favored by Yoda of *Star Wars* fame).

| | |
|---|---|
| English: | Padawan learns a lesson. |
| Japanese equivalent: | **Padawan wa lessun o manabimasu.** |
| | Padawan a lesson learns. |

# Particles

Physicists from Newton on have dabbled in the study of particle theory, and the correct use of particles in the Japanese language is an equally mind-bending study. Books have been written on these tiny but mighty Japanese words. They connect major sentence elements together and help describe subject and object relationships, among other functions. What follows is a quick overview of these pivotal words.

| | |
|---|---|
| **de** | ① Indicates a means. In. By. By means of.<br>② Indicates the place where an action takes place. At. In. |
| **e** | Indicates a destination. |
| **ga** | ① Marks the subject of the sentence. **Ga** is used when the subject is familiar to both speaker and listener.<br>② Used to introduce a new, sometimes contradictory statement. But. |
| **ka** | ① Comes at the end of a sentence, turning that sentence into a question.<br>② Used in midsentence to introduce an option. Or. |
| **mo** | Begs inclusion in the situation. Also. Too. |
| **ne** | Used at the end of a sentence to form a tag question. Isn't it? Don't you think? |
| **ni** | ① Indicates the indirect object of the sentence, or the receiver of a giving/receiving action.<br>② Indicates a destination or goal. To. Toward.<br>③ Indicates the location where something exists. In.<br>④ Indicates time of day, day of week, year, or a specific point in time.<br>⑤ Indicates the doer of an action in a passive sentence. |
| **no** | ① Indicates possession or affiliation. 's. Of.<br>② Turns a noun or nounlike word into a modifier.<br>③ Used at the end of a sentence, it turns the sentence into a question.<br>④ Used at the end of a sentence for emphasis. Slightly feminine. |
| **o** | Indicates the direct object of the sentence. |
| **to** | ① Used to form a list. And.<br>② Indicates the person with whom one does something. With.<br>③ Marks what comes before it as a quote. |
| **wa** | ① は. Introduces what comes before it as the subject or theme of the sentence.<br>② わ. Used at the end of a sentence for emotional resonance. |
| **yo** | Used at the end of a sentence for emphasis. You know? Don't you know? |

# The Basics

## Essentials

MP3

01_01

① **Yes.**

はい。

Hai.

② **No.**

いいえ。

Iie.

③ **Thank you.**

ありがとう。

Arigatō.

④ **No thank you.**

いいえ、けっこうです。

Iie, kekkō desu.

⑤ **You're welcome.**

どういたしまして。

Dō itashimashite.

⑥ **Excuse me!** (apologizing)

すみません!

Sumimasen!

⑦ **Excuse me . . .** (trying to get someone's attention)

あのう、すみません……。

Anō, sumimasen . . .

⑧ **Sorry!**

ごめんなさい!

Gomen nasai!

⑨ **Are you okay?**

だいじょうぶですか?

Daijōbu desu ka?

⑩ **I'm okay.**

だいじょうぶです。

Daijōbu desu.

⑪ **Could you repeat that please?**

もういちど、お願いできますか?

Mō ichido, onegai dekimasu ka?

⑫ **One more time.**

すみません、もういちど……。

Sumimasen, mō ichido . . .

⑬ **Really?**

ほんと?

Honto?

⑭ **I don't understand.**

わかりません。

Wakarimasen.

⑮ **I got it.**

わかりました。

Wakarimashita.

⑯ **Coffee please.**

コーヒーください。

Kōhī kudasai.

⑰ **Let's go.**

行きましょう。

Ikimashō.

⑱ **This is fantastic!**

すごいね！

Sugoi ne!

⑲ **Wait!**

ちょっと待って！

Chotto matte!

⑳ **Help!**

助けて〜！

Tasuketē!

# Meeting and Greeting

MP3

01_02

① **Good morning.**

おはようございます。

Ohayō gozaimasu.

② **Good afternoon.**

こんにちは。
Konnichiwa.

③ **Good evening.**

こんばんは。
Kombanwa.

④ **Pleased to meet you.**

はじめまして、どうぞよろしく。
Hajimemashite, dōzo yoroshiku.

⑤ **The pleasure is mine.**

こちらこそ、どうぞよろしく。
Kochira koso, dōzo yoroshiku.

⑥ **Do you have a minute?**

ちょっと、よろしいですか？
Chotto, yoroshii desuka?

⑦ **Here's my name card.**

わたくし、こういう者です。
よろしくお願いします。
Watakushi, kō iu mono desu.
Yoroshiku onegai shimasu.

⑧ **Nice to see you again.**

どうも、おひさしぶりです。
Dōmo, o-hisashiburi desu.

---

⑨ **How are things?**

調子はどうですか？

Chōshi wa dō desu ka?

---

⑩ **Wonderful weather, isn't it?**

いいお天気ですね。

Ii o-tenki desu ne.

---

# Introducing Yourself

**MP3**
01_03

---

① **I'm Fred Rafferty.**

わたしは、フレッド・ラファティと申します。

Watashi wa, Fureddo Rafati to mōshimasu.

---

② **I'm from San Diego.**

サンディエゴ出身です。

Sandiego shusshin desu.

---

③ **I'm here with Comp-Universe.**

こちらでは、コンプ・ユニバースに
勤めています。

Kochira de wa, Kompu-yunibāsu ni
tsutomete imasu.

---

④ **I'm studying law at Meiji University.**

明治大学で法律を勉強しています。

Meiji Daigaku de hōritsu o benkyō shite imasu.

⑤ **I work in IT.**
ＩＴ関係の仕事をしています。
Ai-tī-kankei no shigoto o shite imasu.

⑥ **I'm just visiting.**
遊びに来ただけです。
Asobi ni kita dake desu.

⑦ **I'm looking for work.** (=I've come to Japan to look for work)
仕事を探しに来ました。
Shigoto o sagashi ni kimashita.

⑧ **I came to Tokyo with my husband.**
夫に付いて東京へ来ました。
Otto ni tsuite Tōkyō e kimashita.

⑨ **I'm teaching English at A-Go.**
エイゴー社で英語を教えています。
Eigōsha de eigo o oshiete imasu.

⑩ **We met last year.**
去年、お会いしましたね。
Kyonen, oai shimashita ne.

# Introducing Others

MP3
01_04

① **Have you two met?**
お二人が会うのは、初めてですか？
O-futari ga au no wa, hajimete desu ka?

② **This is my wife, Sandy.**
妻のサンディです。
Tsuma no Sandī desu.

③ **Is this your daughter?**
お嬢さんですか？
Ojōsan desu ka?

④ **This is Mr. Tanaka, my section chief.**
上司の田中課長です。
Jōshi no Tanaka kachō desu.

⑤ **Let me introduce my husband, Jim.**
紹介します、夫のジムです。
Shōkai shimasu, otto no Jimu desu.

⑥ **I'd like you to meet my friend Kate.**
こちら、友だちのケイトです。
Kochira, tomodachi no Keito desu.

⑦ **My mother wants to meet you.**
母があなたに会いたがっています。
Haha ga anata ni aitagatte imasu.

⑧ **I'm sorry, I've forgotten your name.**
ごめんなさい、お名前を思い出せないのですが。
Gomen nasai, o-namae o omoidasenai no desu ga.

⑨ **Do you have a card?**
お名刺をいただけますか？
O-meishi o itadakemasu ka?

# Exit Lines

01_05

① **Good-bye.**

さようなら。
Sayōnara.

② **Good night.**

おやすみなさい。
Oyasumi nasai.

③ **See you later.**

それじゃ、また。
Soreja, mata.

④ **See ya!**

じゃあね！
Jā ne!

⑤ **See you tomorrow.**

また、あした。
Mata ashita.

⑥ **I've got to go.**

もう行かないと……。
Mō ikanai to . . .

⑦ **My friend is waiting.**

友だちが待ってるんです。
Tomodachi ga matte 'ru n' desu.

⑧ **I need to catch the last train.**

終電に乗りたいので。

Shūden ni noritai no de.

---

⑨ **I'm headed home.**

家に帰るところです。

Ie ni kaeru tokoro desu.

---

⑩ **Let's meet again soon.**

また、近いうちに。

Mata chikai uchi ni.

---

# What? Where?

01_06

---

① **What's your name?**

お名前は？

O-namae wa?

---

② **What time is it?**

いま何時ですか？

Ima nanji desu ka?

---

③ **What is this?**

これは何ですか？

Kore wa nan desu ka?

---

④ **What did you say?**

え？ 何ですか？

E? Nan desu ka?

⑤ **What does this mean?**

これは、どういう意味ですか？

Kore wa dō iu imi desu ka?

⑥ **What's the problem?**

どうしたの？

Dōshita no?

⑦ **Where should we meet?**

どこで待ち合わせする？

Doko de machiawase suru?

⑧ **Where's Meguro?** (Meguro being a neighborhood in Tokyo)

目黒って、どの辺ですか？

Meguro tte, dono hen desu ka?

⑨ **Where's the nearest bank?**

いちばん近くの銀行は、どこですか？

Ichiban chikaku no ginkō wa, doko desu ka?

⑩ **Where are you located?**

住所は、どこですか？

Jūsho wa doko desu ka?

⑪ **Where's the toilet?**

お手洗いは、どこですか？

O-tearai wa doko desu ka?

⑫ **Where are we now?**

ここって、どの辺になりますか？

Koko tte, dono hen ni narimasu ka?

# When? Who?

01_07

① **When's the next train?**
次の電車は何時ですか？
Tsugi no densha wa nanji desu ka?

② **When's the meeting?**
会議は何時からですか？
Kaigi wa nanji kara desu ka?

③ **When should I arrive?**
何時に着けば、いいですか？
Nanji ni tsukeba ii desu ka?

④ **When will we depart?**
出発は何時ですか？
Shuppatsu wa nanji desu ka?

⑤ **When can we talk?**
お話があるんですが、いつなら、いいですか？
O-hanashi ga aru n' desu ga, itsu nara ii desu ka?

⑥ **Who's that?**
あの人、だれ？
Ano hito, dare?

⑦ **Who's in charge?**
責任者は、だれですか？
Sekininsha wa dare desu ka?

⑧ **Who's he talking to?**

彼、だれと話してるの？

Kare, dare to hanashite 'ru no?

⑨ **Whose umbrella is this?**

この傘、だれのですか？

Kono kasa, dare no desu ka?

# Why? How?

**MP3**

**01_08**

① **Why can't I do this?**

どうして、だめなの？

Dōshite, dame na no?

② **Why are we stopping?**

どうして、止まったんですか？

Dōshite, tomatta n' desu ka?

③ **Why do I have to pay this?**

どうして、お金を払わなくちゃ

いけないんですか？

Dōshite, o-kane o harawanakucha
ikenai n' desu ka?

④ **Why not?** (asking why someone won't do something)

なんで？　いいじゃん！

Nande? Ii jan!

⑤ **Why are you upset?**

どうして怒ってるの？

Dōshite okotte 'ru no?

⑥ **How much is this?**

これ、いくらですか？

Kore, ikura desu ka?

⑦ **How do I do that?**

それ、どうやるの？

Sore, dō yaru no?

⑧ **How long does it take?**

時間は、どのくらい、かかりますか？

Jikan wa, dono kurai kakarimasu ka?

⑨ **How are you?**

お元気ですか？

O-genki desu ka?

⑩ **How do I get there?**

どうやって行くの？

Dō yatte iku no?

⑪ **How do you know that?**

どうして、わかるの？

Dōshite wakaru no?

# Can and Need

MP3
01_09

① **I can do it.**

できます。
Dekimasu.

② **I can't do that.**

それは、できません。
Sore wa, dekimasen.

③ **Can I borrow this?**

これ、借りても、いいですか？
Kore, karite mo ii desu ka?

④ **Can I see that?**

それ、見せてもらえますか？
Sore, misete moraemasu ka?

⑤ **Can I get this fixed?**

これ、修理してもらえますか？
Kore, shūri shite moraemasu ka?

⑥ **I need this.**

これは必要です。
Kore wa hitsuyō desu.

⑦ **I don't need that.**

それは、いりません。
Sore wa irimasen.

⑧ **I need a minute.**

ちょっと待ってください。

Chotto matte kudasai.

⑨ **Do we need cash?**

現金が必要ですか？

Genkin ga hitsuyō desu ka?

⑩ **I need another.**

もうひとつ、ください。

Mō hitotsu, kudasai.

# Food, Water, and Shelter

MP3
01_10

① **I'm hungry.**

おなかが、すいています。

Onaka ga suite imasu.

② **I'm thirsty.**

のどが、かわきました。

Nodo ga kawakimashita.

③ **I'm tired.**

疲れています。

Tsukarete imasu.

④ **Can I sleep here?**

ここで寝ても、いいですか？

Koko de nete mo ii desu ka?

⑤ **Do you speak English?**

英語、話せますか？

Eigo, hanasemasu ka?

⑥ **Can I use your bathroom?**

トイレを貸していただけますか？

Toire o kashite itadakemasu ka?

⑦ **Can I use your phone?**

電話を借りても、いいですか？

Denwa o karite mo ii desu ka?

---

### Watakushi wa . . .

A lot of English-speaking students of Japanese trot out the above phrase; it sounds natural in English, but in Japanese it comes off as a slightly stuffy-sounding "as for me." Japanese native speakers avoid this nuance by omitting personal pronouns except when they are necessary, and you can too. Try:

**Watakushi wa Kyoto e ikimasu.**     I'm going to Kyoto.
**→ Kyoto e ikimasu.**     I'm going to Kyoto.

If all you mean to say is, "I'm going to Kyoto," the shorter sentence is perfectly adequate to express your intention. The only time you'll need the **watakushi wa** is when you want to make it absolutely clear that it is you, as opposed to anyone else, who will go to Kyoto, or wherever. "As for me, I'm going to Kyoto."

**Watakushi** is also a starchy option of pronoun from an array of first-person pronouns available to Japanese speakers, among them the less formal **watashi**, the informal, masculine **boku**, and the informal, feminine **atashi**.

# Chapter 2

# Me, Myself, and I

## Family

① **I have a younger sister.**
妹が一人います。
Imōto ga hitori imasu.

② **I'm an only child.**
わたしは一人っ子です。
Watashi wa hitorikko desu.

③ **My brother lives in Chicago.**
兄はシカゴに住んでいます。
Ani wa Shikago ni sunde imasu.

④ **My mom is a teacher.**
母は教師をしています。
Haha wa kyōshi o shite imasu.

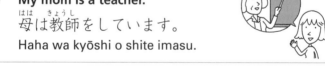

⑤ **My dad is retired.**
父は、もう引退しました。
Chichi wa mō intai shimashita.

⑧ **This is my cousin Jennifer.**
いとこのジェニファーです。
Itoko no Jenifā desu.

**⑦ My family is quite large.**

うちは大家族です。

Uchi wa daikazoku desu.

**⑧ My parents are divorced.**

両親は離婚しました。

Ryōshin wa rikon shimashita.

# Children

MP3
02_02

**① This is my daughter Sophie.**

娘のソフィーです。

Musume no Sofī desu.

**② My son is in first grade.**

息子は小学一年生です。

Musuko wa shōgaku ichinensei desu.

**③ I have three kids.**

子供は3人います。

Kodomo wa sannin imasu.

**④ We don't have kids yet.**

子供は、まだです。

Kodomo wa, mada desu.

**⑤ My oldest child is Sarah.**

いちばん上の子は、サラです。

Ichiban ue no ko wa, Sara desu.

⑥ **My second child is very active.**
二番目の子は、とても活発です。
Nibamme no ko wa, totemo kappatsu desu.

⑦ **My youngest is in kindergarten.**
末っ子は、幼稚園に通っています。
Suekko wa, yōchien ni kayotte imasu.

⑧ **We have twins.**
うちには双子がいます。
Uchi ni wa futago ga imasu.

⑨ **Our kids are grown.**
子供たちは、もう独立しました。
Kodomotachi wa, mō dokuritsu shimashita.

⑩ **We're planning a family.**
子供のことは、これから考えます。
Kodomo no koto wa, kore kara kangaemasu.

# Education

02_03

① **I graduated from UCLA.**
わたしはUCLAを卒業しました。
Watashi wa yū-shī-eru-ē o sotsugyō shimashita.

② **I have a master's in engineering.**
工学の修士号を持っています。
Kōgaku no shūshigō o motte imasu.

**③ I took my BA in sociology at Michigan.**

ミシガン大学で社会学を勉強しました。

Mishigan Daigaku de shakaigaku o benkyō shimashita.

**④ My Ph.D. is in English literature.**

英文学で博士号を取りました。

Eibungaku de hakushigō o torimashita.

**⑤ I'm planning on going back to college.**

もういちど大学に戻ろうかと考えています。

Mō ichido daigaku ni modorō ka to kangaete imasu.

**⑥ I don't have a college degree yet.**

まだ大学を卒業していません。

Mada daigaku o sotsugyō shite imasen.

**⑦ I'm working on my MBA.**

いま、経営学の修士号を取るために勉強中です。

Ima, keieigaku no shūshigō o toru tame ni benkyōchū desu.

**⑧ I majored in philosophy.**

哲学を専攻しました。

Tetsugaku o senkō shimashita.

**⑨ I'm studying now at Waseda.**

いま、早稲田大学で勉強しています。

Ima, Waseda Daigaku de benkyō shite imasu.

**⑩ I'm a high school student.**

高校生です。

Kōkōsei desu.

# Hobbies and Interests

02_04

① **I'm into healthy eating.**

健康食に関心があります。

Kenkōshoku ni kanshin ga arimasu.

② **I like to exercise.**

運動が好きです。

Undō ga suki desu.

③ **I'm a complete foodie.**

わたし、食い道楽なんです。

Watashi, kuidōraku nan desu.

④ **I'm interested in writing.**

ものを書くことに興味があります。

Mono o kaku koto ni kyōmi ga arimasu.

⑤ **I really like traveling.**

旅行が大好きです。

Ryokō ga daisuki desu.

⑥ **I'm a video game fanatic.**

ゲームにはまっています。

Gēmu ni hamatte imasu.

⑦ **I read a lot of manga.**

マンガをたくさん読みます。

Manga o takusan yomimasu.

⑧ **My hobby is collecting art.**

趣味は、美術品の収集です。

Shumi wa, bijutsuhin no shūshū desu.

⑨ **In my free time I like to hang out with friends.**

ひまなときは、友だちと遊んでいます。

Hima na toki wa, tomodachi to asonde imasu.

⑩ **I'm basically an Internet addict.**

わたし、ほとんどネット中毒です。

Watashi, hotondo netto-chūdoku desu.

# Work

02_05

① **I work part-time at a hospital.**

病院でパートをしています。

Byōin de pāto o shite imasu.

② **I'm at Zoni.**

ゾニーに勤めています。

Zonī ni tsutomete imasu.

③ **I'm a homemaker.**

主婦です。

Shufu desu.

④ **I work freelance.**

フリーランスで働いています。

Furīransu de hataraite imasu.

⑤ **I'm looking for work in finance.**

金融関係の仕事を探しています。

Kin'yū-kankei no shigoto o sagashite imasu.

⑥ **I head an import business.**

輸入関係の会社を経営しています。

Yunyū-kankei no kaisha o keiei shite imasu.

⑦ **I own my own company.**

わたしは会社のオーナーです。

Watashi wa kaisha no ōnā desu.

⑧ **I work on a contract basis.**

契約社員として働いています。

Keiyaku-shain toshite hataraite imasu.

⑨ **I'm unemployed.**

いま、失業中です。

Ima, shitsugyōchū desu.

⑩ **I've been laid off.**

リストラされました。

Risutora saremashita.

# Personal History

02_06

① **I was born in Bristol.**

ブリストル生まれです。

Burisutoru umare desu.

② **I've lived all over.**

いろんな国に住んだことがあります。

Ironna kuni ni sunda koto ga arimasu.

③ **This is my first stay in Japan.**

日本は、初めてです。

Nihon wa, hajimete desu.

④ **I grew up in Memphis.**

メンフィスで育ちました。

Menfisu de sodachimashita.

⑤ **My parents are Italian.**

両親はイタリア人です。

Ryōshin wa Itariajin desu.

⑥ **I have roots in France.**

わたしのルーツはフランスです。

Watashi no rūtsu wa Furansu desu.

⑦ **I'm half Japanese, half British.**

わたしは日本人とイギリス人のハーフです。

Watashi wa Nihonjin to Igirisujin no hāfu desu.

⑧ **We used to live in Korea.**

むかし、韓国に住んでいたことがあります。

Mukashi, Kankoku ni sunde ita koto ga arimasu.

⑨ **My home base is in London.**

本拠地はロンドンです。

Honkyochi wa London desu.

Me, Myself, and I

⑩ **I'm adopted.**

わたしは養子です。

Watashi wa yōshi desu.

---

# Likes and Dislikes

02_07

① **I like classical music.**

クラシック音楽が好きです。

Kurashikku ongaku ga suki desu.

---

② **I prefer an honest opinion.**

率直に言ってもらうほうが、いいです。

Sotchoku ni itte morau hō ga, ii desu.

---

③ **I lo–o–o–ove sukiyaki.**

すき焼きは、大、大、大好きです。

Sukiyaki wa, dai-dai-daisuki desu.

---

④ **I'm more into rock than jazz.**

ジャズより、ロックかな。

Jazu yori rokku ka na.

---

⑤ **I don't care for a lot of noise.**

あまり騒がしいのは、ちょっと……。

Amari sawagashii no wa, chotto ...

---

⑥ **I'm not wild about shopping.**

ショッピングは、それほど好きじゃないです。

Shoppingu wa, sorehodo suki ja nai desu.

⑦ **I hate bullies.**

いじめは、許せません。

Ijime wa, yurusemasen.

⑧ **That kind of person makes me sick.**

ああいう人って、むかつく！

Ā iu hito tte, mukatsuku!

⑨ **I can't stand the rainy season.**

梅雨どきの天気って、やだな〜。

Tsuyu-doki no tenki tte ya da nā.

# Personality

MP3
02_08

① **I tend to be cautious.**

わたしは、どちらかというと慎重なタイプです。

Watashi wa, dochiraka to iu to shinchō na taipu desu.

② **I'm relatively open-minded.**

頭は、わりと柔らかいほうじゃないかな。

Atama wa, wari to yawarakai hō ja nai ka na.

③ **I'm an optimist.**

わたしは、楽観的な人間です。

Watashi wa, rakkanteki na ningen desu.

④ **I'm the wait-and-see type.**

わたしは、行動するより見てるタイプです。

Watashi wa, kōdō suru yori mite 'ru taipu desu.

⑤ **I'd say I'm pretty down-to-earth.**

自分では、地に足のついた人間だと
思ってますけど……。

Jibun de wa, chi ni ashi no tsuita ningen da to
omotte 'masu kedo . . .

⑥ **People say I'm hardworking.**

他人からは、努力家だと言われます。

Hito kara wa, doryokuka da to iwaremasu.

⑦ **I'm an easy-going sort.**

わたしは、のんびりタイプの
人間です。

Watashi wa, nombiri taipu no
ningen desu.

⑧ **I can handle almost anything.**

たいていのことは、何とかできますよ。

Taitei no koto wa, nantoka dekimasu yo.

# Values

MP3
02_09

① **Religion is important to me.**

わたしにとって、宗教は大切です。

Watashi ni totte, shūkyō wa taisetsu desu.

② **For me, family comes first.**

わたしの<ruby>場合<rt>ば あい</rt></ruby>、<ruby>家族<rt>か ぞく</rt></ruby>が<ruby>第一<rt>だいいち</rt></ruby>です。

Watashi no baai, kazoku ga daiichi desu.

③ **In a relationship I look for trust and respect.**

わたしが<ruby>人間関係<rt>にんげんかんけい</rt></ruby>に<ruby>求<rt>もと</rt></ruby>めるのは、
<ruby>信頼<rt>しんらい</rt></ruby>と<ruby>尊敬<rt>そんけい</rt></ruby>です。

Watashi ga ningen-kankei ni motomeru no wa,
shinrai to sonkei desu.

④ **I value my friendships.**

わたしは<ruby>友<rt>とも</rt></ruby>だちを<ruby>大切<rt>たいせつ</rt></ruby>にします。

Watashi wa tomodachi o taisetsu ni shimasu.

⑤ **I love my country.**

わたしは<ruby>自分<rt>じ ぶん</rt></ruby>の<ruby>国<rt>くに</rt></ruby>を<ruby>愛<rt>あい</rt></ruby>しています。

Watashi wa jibun no kuni o aishite imasu.

⑥ **I just don't believe in war.**

<ruby>戦争<rt>せんそう</rt></ruby>には、とにかく<ruby>反対<rt>はんたい</rt></ruby>です。

Sensō ni wa, tonikaku hantai desu.

⑦ **Work is one of my top priorities.**

<ruby>仕事<rt>し ごと</rt></ruby>は、わたしにとって<ruby>最優先事項<rt>さいゆうせん じ こう</rt></ruby>の<ruby>一<rt>ひと</rt></ruby>つです。

Shigoto wa, watashi ni totte saiyūsen jikō no hitotsu desu.

⑧ **Music is my life.**

<ruby>音楽<rt>おんがく</rt></ruby>なしの<ruby>人生<rt>じんせい</rt></ruby>なんて、ありえません。

Ongaku nashi no jinsei nante, ariemasen.

# Goals and Aspirations

02_10

① **I have no clue what I want.**

自分がどうしたいのか、
まだ、全然、見えてないんです。

Jibun ga dō shitai no ka,
mada zenzen miete 'nai n' desu.

② **I'd like to start my own company.**

自分で会社を興したいと思っています。

Jibun de kaisha o okoshitai to omotte imasu.

③ **I plan to marry and raise a family.**

結婚して子供を育てたいと思っています。

Kekkon shite kodomo o sodatetai to omotte imasu.

④ **Someday I'm going to be famous.**

いつか、有名になるんだ！

Itsuka, yūmei ni naru n' da!

⑤ **I want to make the world a better place.**

この世界を良くしていく力になりたいです。

Kono sekai o yoku shite iku chikara ni naritai desu.

⑥ **I dream of owning a home.**

自分の家を持つのが夢です。

Jibun no ie o motsu no ga yume desu.

⑦ **I just want to be happy.**

幸せに生きられたら、それでいいんです。

Shiawase ni ikiraretara, sore de ii n' desu.

---

⑧ **I want to travel a lot before settling down.**

独身のうちに、あちこち旅しておきたいな……。

Dokushin no uchi ni, achikochi tabi shite okitai na . . .

---

⑨ **The best plan is no plan.**

計画は白紙にかぎるね！

Keikaku wa hakushi ni kagiru ne!

*Me, Myself, and I*

### All in the Family

One of the cardinal rules in polite Japanese is to avoid putting yourself on a pedestal, inadvertently or otherwise. Therefore, when making family introductions, it's necessary to grasp the specific words used to indicate one's own "humble" family members, as opposed to the members of someone else's family.

|             | SOMEONE ELSE'S | YOUR OWN       |
|-------------|----------------|----------------|
| wife        | **oku-san**    | **kanai, tsuma** |
| husband     | **go-shujin**  | **danna, shujin** |
| child       | **oko-san**    | **uchi no ko** |
| son         | **musuko-san** | **uchi no musuko** |
| daughter    | **musume-san** | **uchi no musume** |
| mother      | **okā-san**    | **haha**       |
| father      | **otō-san**    | **chichi**     |
| aunt        | **oba-san**    | **oba**        |
| uncle       | **oji-san**    | **oji**        |
| grandmother | **obā-san**    | **sobo**       |
| grandfather | **ojī-san**    | **sofu**       |
| cousin      | **itoko-san**  | **uchi no itoko** |

# Chapter 3

# A Time and a Place

## By the Clock

① **What time is it now?**
いま何時ですか？
Ima nanji desu ka?

② **The movie starts at quarter past two.**
映画は2時15分に始まります。
Eiga wa niji jūgofun ni hajimarimasu.

③ **Let's have lunch at noon.**
12時にランチしましょう。
Jūniji ni ranchi shimashō.

④ **Is my watch correct?**
この時計、合ってる？
Kono tokei, atte 'ru?

⑤ **The bar is open till midnight.**
バーは夜中の12時までやっています。
Bā wa yonaka no jūniji made yatte imasu.

⑥ **Our meeting started at half past eleven.**
会議は11時半に始まりました。
Kaigi wa jūichiji-han ni hajimarimashita.

⑦ **We don't work the usual nine-to-five days.**

うちは通常の9時－5時勤務じゃありません。

Uchi wa tsūjō no kuji-goji kimmu ja arimasen.

⑧ **Set your alarm for six A.M.**

目ざまし、6時にかけてね。

Mezamashi, rokuji ni kakete ne.

⑨ **I'm not used to thinking in military time.**

時刻の24時間表示には、慣れてないんです。

Jikoku no nijūyojikan-hyōji ni wa, narete 'nai n' desu.

⑩ **This should take about three hours.**

これは3時間くらい、かかりそうですね。

Kore wa sanjikan kurai kakarisō desu ne.

# Yesterday, Today, and Tomorrow

MP3
03_02

① **I was absent yesterday.**

きのうは欠席しました。

Kinō wa kesseki shimashita.

② **I can't make it today.**

きょうは無理です。

Kyō wa muri desu.

③ **Are you free tomorrow?**

あした、あいてますか？

Ashita, aite 'masu ka?

**④ What day of the month is payday?**

給料日は、毎月何日ですか？

Kyūryōbi wa, maitsuki nannichi desu ka?

**⑤ I haven't seen him for days.**

彼の顔、もう何日も見てないなぁ……。

Kare no kao, mō nannichi mo mite 'nai nā . . .

**⑥ She called the day before yesterday.**

おととい、彼女から電話があったよ。

Ototoi, kanojo kara denwa ga atta yo.

**⑦ I'll pay you back the day after tomorrow.**

あさって、お金返すからね。

Asatte, o-kane kaesu kara ne.

**⑧ I need that report by yesterday!**

その報告書、大至急、出して！

Sono hōkokusho, daishikyū dashite!

**⑨ Tomorrow is another day.**

あしたはあしたの風が吹く。

Ashita wa ashita no kaze ga fuku.

**⑩ Today's the day I've been waiting for.**

待ちに待った日が、やっと来たよ。

Machi ni matta hi ga, yatto kita yo.

**⑪ I read the newspaper every day.**

わたしは毎日、新聞を読みます。

Watashi wa mainichi, shimbun o yomimasu.

# Week In and Week Out

**MP3**
03_03

① **Thank god it's Friday!**
やれやれ、やっと金曜日だ！
Yareyare, yatto Kin'yōbi da!

② **What are your plans for the weekend?**
週末は、どんな予定ですか？
Shūmatsu wa, donna yotei desu ka?

③ **We spend Sundays in the park.**
日曜日は、公園に行ってゆっくり過ごします。
Nichiyōbi wa, kōen ni itte yukkuri sugoshimasu.

④ **Thursday nights I have basketball.**
木曜の夜は、バスケなんだ。
Mokuyō no yoru wa, basuke nan da.

⑤ **Weekdays I work late.**
平日は、夜遅くまで仕事です。
Heijitsu wa, yoru osoku made shigoto desu.

⑥ **Friday nights we eat at home.**
金曜の夜は、家で食事します。
Kin'yō no yoru wa, ie de shokuji shimasu.

⑦ **I have the Monday morning blues.**
月曜の朝は、ゆううつです。
Getsuyō no asa wa, yūutsu desu.

A Time and a Place

⑧ **Saturdays we take care of shopping.**
土曜日には、買い物をまとめてすませます。
Doyōbi ni wa, kaimono o matomete sumasemasu.

⑨ **Wednesday is my day off.**
わたしの休みは、水曜日なんです。
Watashi no yasumi wa, Suiyōbi nan desu.

⑩ **My hair salon is closed on Tuesdays.**
わたしの行きつけの美容室は、火曜定休です。
Watashi no ikitsuke no biyōshitsu wa, Kayō teikyū desu.

## Months and Years

MP3
03_04

① **What year were you born?**
何年生まれですか？
Nannen umare desu ka?

② **January and February are pretty cold in Japan.**
日本の1月と2月は、かなり寒いですね。
Nihon no Ichigatsu to Nigatsu wa, kanari samui desu ne.

③ **March is a busy time of year.**
3月は忙しい時期ですね。
Sangatsu wa isogashii jiki desu ne.

④ **April and May are my favorite months of the year.**
4月と5月は、とくに好きな季節です。
Shigatsu to Gogatsu wa, tokuni suki na kisetsu desu.

⑤ **The rainy season starts in June.**
梅雨入りは、6月ごろです。
Tsuyu-iri wa, Rokugatsu goro desu.

---

⑥ **It tends to be hot in July and August.**
7月、8月は暑くなります。
Shichigatsu, Hachigatsu wa atsuku narimasu.

---

⑦ **September and October are very pleasant.**
9月と10月は、とても過ごしやすい季節です。
Kugatsu to Jūgatsu wa, totemo sugoshiyasui kisetsu desu.

---

⑧ **Fall colors are best in November.**
紅葉の見ごろは11月です。
Kōyō no migoro wa Jūichigatsu desu.

---

⑨ **What holidays do you celebrate in December?**
12月は、何の祝日がありますか？
Jūnigatsu wa, nan no shukujitsu ga arimasu ka?

MP3
03_05

# Next Month, Last Year

① **He's visiting us next month.**
来月、彼が訪ねてくる予定です。
Raigetsu, kare ga tazunete kuru yotei desu.

---

② **We're short on cash this month.**
今月は、ちょっと金欠ぎみなんだ。
Kongetsu wa, chotto kinketsu-gimi nan da.

③ **Last month was busy.**

先月は、忙しかったよ。

Sengetsu wa, isogashikatta yo.

④ **He'll be 20 next year.**

彼は来年20歳です。

Kare wa rainen hatachi desu.

⑤ **We moved here last year.**

去年、こちらへ引っ越してきました。

Kyonen, kochira e hikkoshite kimashita.

⑥ **We'll be here till the year after next.**

再来年まで、こちらに滞在する予定です。

Sarainen made, kochira ni taizai suru yotei desu.

⑦ **This year I plan to study hard.**

今年は本腰を入れて勉強するつもりです。

Kotoshi wa hongoshi o irete benkyō suru tsumori desu.

⑧ **My salary went up this month.**

今月から給料が上がったんだ。

Kongetsu kara kyūryō ga agatta n' da.

⑨ **I'm starting a new job next month.**

F 来月、転職するの。

Raigetsu, tenshoku suru no.

M 来月、転職するんだ。

Raigetsu, tenshoku suru n' da.

⑩ **My electricity bill was expensive last month.**

先月は、電気代が、ずいぶん、かかりました。

Sengetsu wa, denkidai ga zuibun kakarimashita.

---

# Periodically Speaking

MP3
03_06

① **What's the hourly wage here?**

ここの時給は、いくらですか？

Koko no jikyū wa, ikura desu ka?

② **I get up at six A.M. every day.**

わたしは毎朝6時に起きます。

Watashi wa maiasa rokuji ni okimasu.

③ **My monthly payments are too high.**

毎月、生活費がかかりすぎて、きついです。

Maitsuki, seikatsuhi ga kakarisugite, kitsui desu.

④ **Be sure to water the plants from time to time.**

ときどき、植物に水をやってね。

Tokidoki, shokubutsu ni mizu o yatte ne.

⑤ **We travel abroad every summer.**

我が家は、毎年、夏に海外旅行をします。

Wagaya wa, maitoshi, natsu ni kaigai-ryokō o shimasu.

⑥ **I visit my aunt in the hospital once a week.**

週一回、おばの見舞いに行きます。

Shū ikkai, oba no mimai ni ikimasu.

A Time and a Place

⑦ **He sends money home regularly.**
彼は定期的に実家に仕送りしています。
Kare wa teikiteki ni jikka ni shiokuri shite imasu.

# Sooner or Later

MP3
03_07

① **Could you come in earlier tomorrow?**
明日は早めに来ていただけますか？
Asu wa hayame ni kite itadakemasu ka?

② **We can decide that later.**
それは、あとで決めましょう。
Sore wa, ato de kimemashō.

③ **I hope the pizza comes soon.**
ピザ、早く来ないかなぁ。
Piza, hayaku konai ka nā.

④ **We're in a hurry!**
急いでるんです！
Isoideru n' desu!

⑤ **Let's meet after lunch.**
お昼をすませてから、会いましょう。
O-hiru o sumasete kara, aimashō.

⑥ **Let's compare notes before the meeting.**
会議の前に、意見のすりあわせをしておきましょう。
Kaigi no mae ni, iken no suriawase o shite okimashō.

⑦ **I want to get there early.**

わたしは早めに着いておきたいです。

Watashi wa hayame ni tsuite okitai desu.

⑧ **This might take a while.**

これは、ちょっと時間がかかるかもね。

Kore wa, chotto jikan ga kakaru ka mo ne.

⑨ **I'm going to be late!**

まずい、遅れそう！

Mazui, okuresō!

⑩ **He'll get here sooner or later.**

彼、そのうち来ると思うよ。

Kare, sono uchi kuru to omou yo.

# Timely Remarks

MP3
03_08

① **Just in the nick of time!**

ギリギリ間に合ったね！

Girigiri ma ni atta ne!

② **Maybe next time.**

また、こんど。

Mata kondo.

③ **This is okay for the time being.**

とりあえず、これでいいよ。

Toriaezu, kore de ii yo.

④ **Time flies.**
時がたつのは早いですね。
Toki ga tatsu no wa hayai desu ne.

⑤ **Good timing!**
グッド・タイミング！
Guddo taimingu!

⑥ **Time's up!**
時間です。
Jikan desu.

⑦ **Take your time.**
ごゆっくり、どうぞ。
Go-yukkuri, dōzo.

⑧ **Please be on time.**
時間厳守でお願いします。
Jikan genshu de onegai shimasu.

# The Time of Your Life

03_09

① **Things were tough when I was a student.**
学生時代は、生活が苦しかったです。
Gakusei jidai wa, seikatsu ga kurushikatta desu.

② **I was pretty wild in my twenties.**
二十代は、かなり遊んでいました。
Nijūdai wa, kanari asonde imashita.

③ **He's over the hill.**

彼、中年くさくなったね。

Kare, chūnen-kusaku natta ne.

④ **She's thirty-something.**

彼女、三〇いくつ、ってところかな。

Kanojo, sanjū-ikutsu tte tokoro ka na.

⑤ **I'm looking at retirement.**

退職も、そう遠くないからね。

Taishoku mo, sō tōkunai kara ne.

⑥ **I had an ideal childhood.**

わたしは理想的な子供時代を過ごしました。

Watashi wa risōteki na kodomo-jidai o sugoshimashita.

⑦ **He's having a midlife crisis.**

彼は「中年の危機」まっただ中です。

Kare wa "chūnen no kiki" mattadanaka desu.

⑧ **You've got your whole life ahead of you.**

人生、これからだよ！

Jinsei, kore kara da yo!

# A Matter of Timing

MP3
03_10

① **Slow and steady wins the race.**

急がば回れ。

Isogaba maware.

**A Time and a Place**

② **Some people watch TV 24/7.**

明けても暮れてもテレビ漬け、
みたいな人もいますね。

Akete mo kurete mo terebi-zuke,
mitai na hito mo imasu ne.

③ **We don't have all day.**

時間がないんです、早くしてください。

Jikan ga nai n' desu, hayaku shite kudasai.

④ **I'll be right back!**

すぐ戻ります。

Sugu modorimasu.

⑤ **Let's wait and see.**

しばらく、ようすを見ようよ。

Shibaraku, yōsu o miyō yo.

⑥ **Get a move on!**

早く！

Hayaku!

⑦ **Strike while the iron's hot!**

鉄は熱いうちに打て。

Tetsu wa atsui uchi ni ute.

⑧ **Get a life!**

しっかりしなよ！

Shikkari shina yo!

## Drugstore Items

04_01

① **Do you carry Q-tips?**

綿棒は置いてありますか？

Membō wa oite arimasu ka?

② **Where are the tampons?**

タンポンは、どこにありますか？

Tampon wa, doko ni arimasu ka?

③ **I need a dandruff shampoo.**

フケ取りシャンプーがほしいんですけど。

Fuketori shampū ga hoshii n' desu kedo.

④ **What do you recommend for athlete's foot?**

水虫には、どの薬がいいですか？

Mizumushi ni wa, dono kusuri ga ii desu ka?

⑤ **How do I use this?**

これは、どうやって使うんですか？

Kore wa dō yatte tsukau n' desu ka?

⑥ **Can you give me something to help me sleep?**

不眠に効く薬、ありますか？

Fumin ni kiku kusuri, arimasu ka?

⑦ **What does this do?**

これは、どんな効き目があるんですか?

Kore wa, donna kikime ga aru n' desu ka?

⑧ **Does this have caffeine in it?**

この薬、カフェインがはいってますか?

Kono kusuri, kafein ga haitte 'masu ka?

⑨ **I need aspirin.**

アスピリンをください。

Asupirin o kudasai.

⑩ **What's best for sore muscles?**

筋肉痛には、どの薬がいちばん

よく効きますか?

Kinniku-tsū ni wa, dono kusuri ga ichiban
yoku kikimasu ka?

# Groceries

MP3

04_02

① **Where's the shortening?**

ショートニングは、どこですか?

Shōtoningu wa, doko desu ka?

② **Are you out of eggs?**

タマゴは売り切れですか?

Tamago wa urikire desu ka?

③ **Do you deliver?**

配達、してもらえますか？
はいたつ

Haitatsu, shite moraemasu ka?

④ **Do you have Raisin Bran?**

「レーズン・ブラン」、ありますか？

"Rēzun Buran" arimasu ka?

⑤ **I have an eco-bag.**

レジ袋は、いりません。
ぶくろ

Rejibukuro wa irimasen.

⑥ **Is this organic?**

これ、有機栽培ですか？
ゆう き さいばい

Kore, yūki-saibai desu ka?

⑦ **Where is this from?**

この産地は、どこですか？
さん ち

Kono sanchi wa, doko desu ka?

⑧ **Is this local produce?**

これ、地元でとれたものですか？
じ もと

Kore, jimoto de toreta mono desu ka?

⑨ **What's the difference between these?**

それとこれは、どこがちがうんですか？

Sore to kore wa, doko ga chigau n desu ka?

⑩ **What is the expiration date?**

賞味期限は？
しょう み き げん

Shōmi-kigen wa?

# Furniture

MP3
04_03

① **I'm looking for a sofa bed.**

ソファ・ベッドを探してるんですけど……。

Sofā-beddo o sagashite 'ru n' desu kedo . . .

② **Do you have an extralong bed?**

エクストラ・ロング・サイズのベッド、ありますか？

Ekusutora-rongu-saizu no beddo, arimasu ka?

③ **Can I put this on tatami?**

これ、畳の上に置いても、だいじょうぶですか？

Kore, tatami no ue ni oitemo daijōbu desu ka?

④ **I want a desk made of solid wood.**

むく材の机がほしいんです。

Mukuzai no tsukue ga hoshii n' desu.

⑤ **What are the dimensions?**

寸法は？

Sumpō wa?

⑥ **I need a table that seats six.**

6人がけのテーブルが

ほしいんです。

Rokunin-gake no tēburu ga
hoshii n' desu.

⑦ **I need an office chair with back support.**

背もたれ付きのオフィス・チェアを探しています。

Semotare-tsuki no ofisu-cheā o sagashite imasu.

# Clothing Styles

04_04

① **I need an interview suit.**

面接用のスーツがほしいんですが。

Mensetsu-yō no sūtsu ga hosii n' desu ga.

② **Do you have anything more hip?**

もっとイケてる感じの、
ありませんか？

Motto iketeru kanji no,
arimasen ka?

③ **I'm looking for a business suit.**

ビジネス・スーツを探しています。

Bijinesu sūtsu o sagashite imasu.

④ **I just want something really hot.**

とにかく、思いっきりセクシーなのが、ほしいんです。

Tonikaku, omoikkiri sekushī na no ga, hoshii n' desu.

⑤ **This color doesn't really suit me.**

この色、わたしには似合いませんね。

Kono iro, watashi ni wa niaimasen ne.

⑥ **I want something like this.**

こういう感じ<ruby>感<rt>かん</rt></ruby>じのが、ほしいんです。

Kō iu kanji no ga, hoshii n' desu.

⑦ **Do you have cotton dress shirts?**

コットンのワイシャツ、ありますか？

Kotton no waishatsu, arimasu ka?

⑧ **What goes well with this?**

これと合わせるには、何がいいですか？

Kore to awaseru ni wa, nani ga ii desu ka?

⑨ **I need something for a black-tie event.**

フォーマルなイベントに着ていく
服がいるんです。

Fōmaru na ibento ni kite iku
fuku ga iru n' desu.

⑩ **How about something less flashy?**

もう少しおとなしい感じのは、ありませんか？

Mō sukoshi otonashii kanji no wa, arimasen ka?

# Clothing Sizes and Materials

MP3
04_05

① **Do you have tall sizes?**

トール・サイズは、ありますか？

Tōru-saizu wa, arimasu ka?

② **Do you carry extralarge shoes?**

大きいサイズの靴は、ありますか？

Ōkii saizu no kutsu wa, arimasu ka?

③ **Can you do alterations?**

お直しは、できますか？

O-naoshi wa, dekimasu ka?

④ **This feels too snug.**

ちょっと、ぴったりしすぎですね。

Chotto, pittari shisugi desu ne.

⑤ **What is this made of?**

これ、素材は何ですか？

Kore, sozai wa nan desu ka?

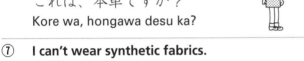

⑥ **Is this genuine leather?**

これは、本革ですか？

Kore wa, hongawa desu ka?

⑦ **I can't wear synthetic fabrics.**

化繊はダメなんです。

Kasen wa dame nan desu.

⑧ **Do you have this in my size?**

これ、わたしに合うサイズはありますか？

Kore, watashi ni au saizu wa arimasu ka?

⑨ **Is this machine-washable?**

これ、洗濯機で洗えますか？

Kore, sentakki de araemasu ka?

⑩ **Will this shrink after I wash it?**

これ、洗濯したら縮みますか？

Kore, sentaku shitara chijimimasu ka?

# Electronics

MP3

04_06

① **I need a wireless router.**

無線ルータを探しています。

Musen-rūta o sagashite imasu.

② **Which of these TVs has the sharpest picture?**

どのテレビが、いちばんきれいですか？

Dono terebi ga ichiban kirei desu ka?

③ **Do you sell region-free DVD players?**

リージョン・フリーのＤＶＤプレーヤー、

ありますか？

Rījon-furī no dī-bui-dī-purēyā,
arimasu ka?

④ **Is this software only in Japanese?**

このソフト、日本語しかありませんか？

Kono sofuto, Nihongo shika arimasen ka?

⑤ **Which is your fastest laptop?**

ラップトップでいちばん速いのは、どれですか？

Rapputoppu de ichiban hayai no wa, dore desu ka?

⑥ **Can you help set it up?**

セット・アップも、お願いできますか?

Setto-appu mo, onegai dekimasu ka?

---

⑦ **Do I need a transformer to use this abroad?**

これを外国で使うには、変圧器がいりますか?

Kore o gaikoku de tsukau ni wa, hen'atsuki ga irimasu ka?

---

⑧ **Is this sold only in Japan?**

これは、日本でしか売っていないものですか?

Kore wa, Nihon de shika utte inai mono desu ka?

---

⑨ **Does this come with English instructions?**

英語の説明書は、付いてますか?

Eigo no setsumeisho wa, tsuite 'masu ka?

---

⑩ **I'm looking for a high-end stereo system.**

システム・ステレオのハイエンド・モデルを
探してるんですけど。

Shisutemu-sutereo no haiendo-moderu o
sagashite 'ru n' desu kedo.

---

# Appliances

MP3
04_07

① **We want an energy-efficient refrigerator.**

省エネ型の冷蔵庫を買いたいんですけど。

Shōenegata no reizōko o kaitai n' desu kedo.

**②** **Do you carry induction-heating stoves?**

ＩＨクッキング・ヒーターは、ありますか？

Ai-etchi-kukkingu-hītā wa, arimasu ka?

---

**③** **I want a powerful vacuum cleaner.**

強力な掃除機がほしいんです。

Kyōryoku na sōjiki ga hoshii n' desu.

---

**④** **What are the advantages of this oven?**

このオーブンは、どんな特長がありますか？

Kono ōbun wa, donna tokuchō ga arimasu ka?

---

**⑤** **Is this rice-cooker easy to use?**

この炊飯器、使い方は簡単ですか？

Kono suihanki, tsukaikata wa kantan desu ka?

---

**⑥** **I want a clothes dryer that's fast and quiet.**

速くて静かな乾燥機がほしいんですけど。

Hayakute shizuka na kansōki ga hoshii n' desu kedo.

---

**⑦** **What is the capacity of this washing machine?**

この洗濯機、何キロまで洗えますか？

Kono sentakki, nankiro made araemasu ka?

---

**⑧** **How long is the warranty?**

保証は何年ですか？

Hoshō wa nannen desu ka?

---

**⑨** **Can you deliver it today?**

きょう配達してもらえますか？

Kyō haitatsu shite moraemasu ka?

⑩ **Can you take away the old one?**

古いのを引き取ってもらえますか？

Furui no o hikitotte moraemasu ka?

# Beauty Products

MP3
04_08

① **I need a light moisturizer.**

さっぱりタイプの保湿液がほしいんですけど。

Sappari taipu no hoshitsueki ga hoshii n' desu kedo.

② **Do you carry a natural facial cleanser?**

天然成分のクレンジングは、ありますか？

Tennen seibun no kurenjingu wa, arimasu ka?

③ **Is this foundation okay for oily skin?**

このファンデーションは、

オイリー・スキンでもだいじょうぶですか？

Kono fandēshon wa,
oirī-sukin demo daijōbu desu ka?

④ **Which sunblock do you recommend?**

どの日焼け止めがおすすめですか？

Dono hiyakedome ga osusume desu ka?

⑤ **I need a hypoallergenic soap.**

アレルギーを起こしにくい石鹸をください。

Arerugī o okoshinikui sekken o kudasai.

⑥ **I'm looking for a gentle toner.**

敏感な肌に合う化粧水を探してるんですけど。

Binkan na hada ni au keshōsui o sagashite 'ru n' desu kedo.

---

⑦ **Will this dry out my skin?**

これだと、肌がカサカサになっちゃいますか？

Koredato, hada ga kasakasa ni natchaimasu ka?

---

⑧ **I'd like a long-lasting lipstick.**

落ちにくい口紅をください。

Ochinikui kuchibeni o kudasai.

---

⑨ **Is this mascara water-soluble?**

このマスカラは水溶性ですか？

Kono masukara wa suiyōsē desu ka?

---

⑩ **I need something to clear up my skin.**

何か、肌荒れに効くものは、ありますか？

Nanika, hadaare ni kiku mono wa, arimasu ka?

---

# Art and Antiques

MP3
04_09

① **Can I pick this up and look at it?**

これ、手に取ってみても、いいですか？

Kore, te ni totte mite mo, ii desu ka?

---

② **When was this made?**

これは、いつごろ作られたものですか？

Kore wa, itsugoro tsukurareta mono desu ka?

③ **Where does this come from?**

どこから来たものですか？

Doko kara kita mono desu ka?

④ **Is that your lowest price?**

これ以上は安くなりませんか？

Kore ijō wa yasuku narimasen ka?

⑤ **Does this have its original box?**

これ、共箱付きですか？

Kore, tomobako-tsuki desu ka?

⑥ **Is this work signed by the artist?**

作者の名入りですか？

Sakusha no na-iri desu ka?

⑦ **What was this used for?**

これは、何に使ったものですか？

Kore wa, nan ni tsukatta mono desu ka?

⑧ **Is this a flaw?**

これ、傷ですか？

Kore, kizu desu ka?

⑨ **Is this a one-of-a-kind original?**

これは、一点ものですか？

Kore wa, itten-mono desu ka?

⑩ **Does the price include the frame?**

これは、額縁も入れた値段ですか？

Kore wa, gakubuchi mo ireta nedan desu ka?

# Gifts and Traditional Items

MP3
04_10

① **Do you have any yukata in big sizes?**

大きいサイズのゆかたは、ありますか？

Ōkii saizu no yukata wa, arimasu ka?

② **Where can I find modern woodblock prints?**

現代作家の木版画は、どこで買えますか？

Gendai-sakka no mokuhanga wa, doko de kaemasu ka?

③ **How old is this chest?**

このたんすは、どれくらい古いものですか？

Kono tansu wa, dorekurai furui mono desu ka?

④ **Are these fans hand-painted or printed?**

この扇子は、手描きですか？　印刷ですか？

Kono sensu wa, tegaki desu ka? Insatsu desu ka?

⑤ **Can you gift-wrap these chopsticks please?**

この箸、ギフト用に包んでもらえますか？

Kono hashi, gifuto-yō ni tsutsunde moraemasu ka?

⑥ **I want to send this pottery abroad.**

この陶器、外国に送りたいんですけど。

Kono tōki, gaikoku ni okuritai n' desu kedo.

⑦ **How should I care for this lacquerware?**

この漆塗り、手入れは、どうすればいいですか？

Kono urushinuri, te-ire wa, dō sureba ii desu ka?

⑧ **What does this kanji mean here?**

ここに書いてある漢字は、どういう意味ですか？

Koko ni kaite aru kanji wa, dō iu imi desu ka?

⑨ **I'm looking for cool new gadgets.**

ちょっと気のきいた小物を探してるんですけど。

Chotto ki no kiita komono o sagashite 'ru n' desu kedo.

⑩ **Can you show me how to wear this?**

どうやって着るのか、教えてもらえますか？

Dō yatte kiru no ka, oshiete moraemasu ka?

# Payment

MP3
04_11

① **Can I pay with a credit card?**

クレジット・カードは使えますか？

Kurejitto-kādo wa tsukaemasu ka?

② **I'd like to pay cash for these.**

現金で支払います。

Genkin de shiharaimasu.

③ **Can you send this to my home?**

これ、自宅へ配送してもらえますか？

Kore, jitaku e haisō shite moraemasu ka?

④ **I want to send these to a friend.**

これ、友人あてに発送してほしいんですけど。

Kore, yūjin-ate ni hassō shite hoshii n' desu kedo.

**Shopping**

⑤ **Can you hold this for me?**

これ、取り置きしといてもらえますか？

Kore, torioki shitoite moraemasu ka?

⑥ **Am I allowed to ship this abroad?**

海外向けに発送しても、だいじょうぶですか？

Kaigaimuke ni hassō shite mo, daijōbu desu ka?

⑦ **Could you write me a receipt?**

領収書をください。

Ryōshūsho o kudasai.

---

### Shopping

Tip one: In this chapter, you may have noticed that the main verb forms you'll need while shopping are **arimasu ka** (Do you have . . . ?), **hoshii n' desu** (I want/need . . .), and **kudasai** (May I have . . . ?). In fact, assuming you can see what you want, and your finger is working, you could survive by simply pointing and requesting: **Sore, kudasai** (I want that).

Tip Two: Finding what you want first requires finding the store in which it's sold. For reference, here's a list of the major stores that you might need to access. Simply ask, (shop type) **wa doko desu ka?**

| | | |
|---|---|---|
| bakery | **pan'ya** | パン屋 |
| convenience store | **kombini** | コンビニ |
| department store | **depāto** | デパート |
| drugstore | **yakkyoku** | 薬局 |
| electronics store | **denkiya** | 電気屋 |
| florist | **hanaya** | 花屋 |
| grocery store | **sūpā** | スーパー |
| hardware store | **hōmusentā** | ホームセンター |
| stationery store | **bunbōguten** | 文房具店 |

## Getting Directions

**05_01**

① **Where's the nearest post office?**

いちばん近くの郵便局は、

どこですか？

Ichiban chikaku no yūbinkyoku wa,
doko desu ka?

② **Can you draw me a map?**

地図を描いてもらえませんか？

Chizu o kaite moraemasen ka?

③ **Is there a cash machine around here?**

この近くにＡＴＭはありますか？

Kono chikaku ni ē-tī-emu wa arimasu ka?

④ **Are we in Ginza?**

ここは銀座ですか？

Koko wa Ginza desu ka?

⑤ **How long does it take to get there by train?**

そこへ行くのに、電車で何分かかりますか？

Soko e iku no ni, densha de nampun kakarimasu ka?

⑥ **Can you give me a landmark?**

何か目印になるものは、ありますか？

Nanika mejirushi ni naru mono wa, arimasu ka?

⑦ **I'm totally lost!**

完全に道に迷ってしまいました。

Kanzen ni michi ni mayotte shimaimashita.

⑧ **Can you direct me from Roppongi Crossing?**

六本木の交差点から、どう行けばいいですか？

Roppongi no Kōsaten kara, dō ikeba ii desu ka?

⑨ **I think I took a wrong turn . . .**

曲がり角、まちがえたかな……。

Magarikado, machigaeta ka na . . .

⑩ **Would you please show me the way?**

道順を教えていただけませんか？

Michijun o oshiete itadakemasen ka?

# Giving Directions

MP3

05_02

① **Turn right at the gas station.**

ガソリンスタンドを右へ曲がってください。

Gasorinsutando o migi e magatte kudasai.

② **Take your first left, then go straight.**

最初の角を左へ曲がって、あとは、まっすぐです。

Saishono kado o hidari e magatte, ato wa, massugu desu.

③ **Go past two traffic lights and stop at the next street you come to.**

信号を二つ通り越して、次の角のところで
止めてください。

Shingō o futatsu tōrikoshite, tsugi no kado no tokoro de tomete kudasai.

④ **It's the building diagonal to the shrine.**

神社の斜め向かいのビルです。

Jinja no nanamemukai no biru desu.

⑤ **It's right there, across the street.**

すぐそこ、通りを渡ったところですよ。

Sugu soko, tōri o watatta tokoro desu yo.

⑥ **Turn right at the second street, which is a dead end.**

二本目の道を右に曲がってください。
行き止まりの道ですけど。

Nihomme no michi o migi ni magatte kudasai.
Ikidomari no michi desu kedo.

⑦ **Go up the slope and you'll see a parking lot.**

坂をのぼっていくと、駐車場が見えるはずです。

Saka o nobotte iku to, chūshajō ga mieru hazu desu.

⑧ **Our house is on the northwestern side of the park.**

うちは、公園の北西側になります。

Uchi wa, kōen no hokuseigawa ni narimasu.

⑨ **Our company is next to the cinema.**
うちの会社は、映画館のとなりです。
Uchi no kaisha wa, eigakan no tonari desu.

## Train and Subway

**05_03**

① **Where do I buy tickets?**
切符売り場は、どこですか？
Kippu uriba wa doko desu ka?

② **Is this the Ginza Line?**
これ、銀座線ですか？
Kore, Ginza-sen desu ka?

③ **I'd like two reserved seats to Nagoya.**
名古屋まで、指定席2枚。
Nagoya made, shiteiseki nimai.

④ **Is it faster going by subway or train?**
地下鉄と電車と、どっちが早いですか？
Chikatetsu to densha to, dotchi ga hayai desu ka?

⑤ **Do I need to transfer?**
乗り換えは、ありますか？
Norikae wa, arimasu ka?

⑥ **Is this train headed toward Wakoshi?**
この電車は、和光市行きですか？
Kono densha wa, Wakōshi-yuki desu ka?

⑦ **Could you tell me what the next stop is?**

次は何という駅ですか？

Tsugi wa nan to iu eki desu ka?

---

⑧ **Can I use this pass on the JR?**

このカードでＪＲに乗れますか？

Kono kādo de Jē-āru ni noremasu ka?

---

⑨ **Where's the lost and found?**

落とし物センターは、どこですか？

Otoshimono-sentā wa doko desu ka?

---

## Buses and Taxis

MP3
05_04

---

① **Does bus 92 stop here?**

92番のバスは、ここに止まりますか？

Kyūjūni-ban no basu wa, koko ni tomarimasu ka?

---

② **Does this bus stop near Shinjuku Park?**

このバスは、新宿公園の近くに
止まりますか？

Kono basu wa, Shinjuku Kōen no chikaku ni
tomarimasu ka?

---

③ **Can you tell me when we're near Jingumae?**

神宮前に近くなったら、教えてもらえませんか？

Jingūmae ni chikaku nattara, oshiete moraemasen ka?

④　**Excuse me, do you know when the next bus will come?**

すみません、次のバスは何時ごろでしょうか？

Sumimasen, tsugi no basu wa nanji goro deshō ka?

⑤　**How do I get the driver to stop?**

バス停で止まってほしいときは、

どうすればいいんでしょうか？

Basutei de tomatte hoshii toki wa,
dō sureba ii n' deshō ka?

⑥　**Take me to the Imperial Hotel.**

帝国ホテルまで。

Teikoku Hoteru made.

⑦　**I need to get to Haneda immediately.**

羽田まで、大急ぎでお願いします。

Haneda made, ōisogi de onegai shimasu.

⑧　**Here's a map and phone number.**

これ、目的地の地図と電話番号です。

Kore, mokutekichi no chizu to denwa-bangō desu.

⑨　**Please use Aoyama Avenue.**

青山通りを通ってください。

Aoyama Dōri o tōtte kudasai.

⑩　**Okay, let me out here.**

ありがとう、ここでけっこうです。

Arigatō, koko de kekkō desu.

# Cars and Roads

MP3
05_05

① **I'd like to rent a car.**

レンタカーを借りたいんですけど。

Rentakā o karitai n' desu kedo.

② **Fill 'er up.**

満タンで。

Mantan de.

③ **Where can I find parking around here?**

このあたりだと、駐車場はどこにありますか？

Kono atari da to, chūshajō wa doko ni arimasu ka?

④ **You can't turn right from this lane.**

この車線は、右折禁止ですよ。

Kono shasen wa, usetsu-kinshi desu yo.

⑤ **What does that sign there mean?**

あの標識は、どういう意味ですか？

Ano hyōshiki wa, dō iu imi desu ka?

⑥ **Oh no! My car's been towed!**

しまった！ 車、レッカー移動された！

Shimatta! Kuruma, rekkā-idō sareta!

⑦ **The streets are so narrow here!**

このへんの道路は狭いですね！

Kono hen no dōro wa semai desu ne!

⑧ **My license has expired**

免許の期限、切れちゃった。

Menkyo no kigen, kirechatta.

⑨ **I can't drive tonight because I've been drinking.**

きょうはお酒を飲んだので、運転はできません。

Kyō wa o-sake o nonda no de, unten wa dekimasen.

⑩ **Your driving sucks.**

ひどい運転だね。

Hidoi unten da ne.

# Bicycles and Motorcycles

MP3
05_06

① **Can I lock my bike here?**

自転車、ここにロックでつないで

いいですか？

Jitensha, koko ni rokku de tsunaide
ii desu ka?

② **I have an extra helmet if you want a ride.**

後ろに乗る？　ヘルメット、あるよ。

Ushiro ni noru? Herumetto, aru yo.

③ **Is it okay to park here?**

ここに止めても、だいじょうぶ？

Koko ni tomete mo, daijōbu?

④ **My bike's been stolen.** (telling a police officer)
自転車を盗まれました。
Jitensha o nusumaremashita.

⑤ **Sorry officer, I seem to have left my registration at home.**
すみません、車検証は家に
置いてきてしまいました。
Sumimasen, shakenshō wa ie ni
oite kite shimaimashita.

⑥ **I think my brakes are going.**
ブレーキがきかなくなってるみたい。
Burēki ga kikanaku natte 'ru mitai.

⑦ **Where can I get a flat tire repaired?**
タイヤのパンク修理は、
どこでやってもらえますか？
Taiya no panku-shūri wa,
doko de yatte moraemasu ka?

⑧ **I'd like to get an electric bike.**
電動自転車、ほしいな。
Dendō-jitensha, hoshii na.

⑨ **I use this for commuting to work.**
これは、通勤用に使っています。
Kore wa, tsūkin-yō ni tsukatte imasu.

# Airplanes and Airports

MP3
05_07

① **We'd like to book roundtrip tickets to Fukuoka.**

福岡までの往復航空券を
予約したいんですけど。

Fukuoka made no ōfuku-kōkūken o
yoyaku shitai n' desu kedo.

② **Is that a direct flight?**

直行便ですか？

Chokkōbin desu ka?

③ **Do I need a visa to fly there?**

そこへ行くには、ビザが必要ですか？

Soko e iku ni wa, biza ga hitsuyō desu ka?

④ **Do you have any special packages or discounts?**

パック旅行とか、

ディスカウント・キャンペーンとか、ありますか？

Pakku ryokō toka,
disukaunto-kyampēn toka, arimasu ka?

⑤ **By what time should I arrive at the airport?**

何時までに空港に着いていればいいですか？

Nanji made ni kūkō ni tsuite ireba ii desu ka?

⑥ **Is my flight, JAL 001, leaving on schedule?**

ＪＡＬの００１便、定刻の出発ですか？

Jaru no zero-zero-ichi-bin, teikoku no shuppatsu desu ka?

⑦ **I'd like an aisle seat.**

通路側の席をお願いします。

Tsūrogawa no seki o onegai shimasu.

⑧ **My flight's been delayed.**

わたしが乗る飛行機、遅れてるんです。

Watashi ga noru hikōki, okurete 'ru n' desu.

⑨ **We just landed.**

いま、到着したところです。

Ima, tōchaku shita tokoro desu.

⑩ **Can you wait for me outside Immigration?**

入国審査を出たところで待っててくれますか？

Nyūkoku-shinsa o deta tokoro de matte 'te kuremasu ka?

## Boats and Ferries

MP3

05_08

① **When's the next boat?**

次の出航は何時ですか？

Tsugi no shukkō wa nanji desu ka?

② **How much does the ferry cost?**

フェリーの料金は、いくらですか？

Ferī no ryōkin wa, ikura desu ka?

③ **I get seasick.**

わたし、船酔いする性質なんです。

Watashi, funayoi suru tachi nan desu.

④ **Is the crossing very rough?**

船はかなり揺れますか？

Fune wa kanari yuremasu ka?

⑤ **Can we sit on the deck?**

デッキ席、ありますか？

Dekki-seki, arimasu ka?

# On Foot

MP3

05_09

① **Let's hoof it for a change.**

たまには歩こうよ。

Tamani wa arukō yo.

② **Is it within walking distance?**

歩いていける距離ですか？

Aruite ikeru kyori desu ka?

③ **How far is it from here to the station?**

ここから駅まで、どのくらいありますか？

Koko kara eki made, dono kurai arimasu ka?

④ **I'm getting blisters.**

足にマメができかけてるんです。

Ashi ni mame ga dekikakete 'ru n' desu.

⑤ **It's hard to maneuver through these crowds.**

この人ごみの<ruby>中<rt>なか</rt></ruby>を<ruby>歩<rt>ある</rt></ruby>くのは、

たいへんだね。

Kono hitogomi no naka o aruku nowa,
taihen da ne.

## Verb Forms

Students of the Japanese language usually encounter the dictionary form of a verb first, and then the "masu form." The dictionary form of **iku**, for example, becomes in masu form, **ikimasu**. Similarly, the verb **kuru** becomes **kimasu**, and **kaeru** becomes **kaerimasu**. The dictionary form is considered casual, and acceptable to use among close friends and family. The masu form, however, is a safely polite verb form—neither ultra-formal nor too relaxed.

You might ask your brother out to a concert like this: **Konsāto ni iku?** But you would ask a co-worker the same question like this: **Konsāto ni ikimasu ka?**

Some entries in this book give masu-form equivalents when the English sentence itself is polite. But elsewhere, the same verb may appear in the dictionary form, or in another plain form, to convey an aggressive, conversational, or urgent tone. So, for example, **ikimashita**, **kimashita** or **kaerimashita** might become **itta**, **kita**, or **kaetta**.

We have worked hard to match each English sentence with its most natural Japanese equivalent, down to the form of the verb used, so that you don't end up sounding stuffy, stilted, or slovenly. Judging precisely which verb form best matches the tone of each phrase is not an exact science, and there are several phrases that could dress up or down, but we have tried to imagine the situation in which you would most likely use each phrase and to apply the appropriate verb to convey the correct nuance.

## Scoping Out the Place

① **I've heard this place is great.**

このお店、おいしいって評判ですよ。

Kono o-mise, oishii tte hyōban desu yo.

② **Want to give this place a try?**

この店にしてみようか？

Kono mise ni shite miyō ka?

③ **Can we make reservations for lunch?**

ランチの予約、できますか？

Ranchi no yoyaku, dekimasu ka?

④ **I'd like to make reservations for four at seven o'clock tonight.**

今夜7時に4人、予約をお願いします。

Kon'ya shichiji ni yonin, yoyaku o onegai shimasu.

⑤ **Can we reserve the entire restaurant?**

貸切はできますか？

Kashikiri wa dekimasu ka?

⑥ **We'd like a table outside, please.**

外のテーブルをお願いします。

Soto no tēburu o onegai shimasu.

⑦ **Do you have a smoking section?**

喫煙席は、ありますか？

Kitsuenseki wa, arimasu ka?

⑧ **How long is the wait?**

待ち時間は、どのくらいですか？

Machijikan wa, dono kurai desu ka?

# Ordering

MP3
06_02

① **May I see a menu?**

メニューを見せていただけますか？

Menyū o misete itadakemasu ka?

② **What are today's specials?**

きょうのスペシャル・メニューは？

Kyō no supesharu-menyū wa?

③ **What do you recommend?**

どれが、おすすめですか？

Dore ga, osusume desu ka?

④ **I need a bit more time to decide.**

もう少し待ってください。

Mō sukoshi matte kudasai.

⑤ **We're ready to order now.**

注文をお願いします。

Chūmon o onegai shimasu.

⑥ **I'll take the lunch set.**

ランチ・セットにします。

Ranchi-setto ni shimasu.

⑦ **I'll have what they're having.**

あちらのテーブルと同じ料理をお願いします。

Achira no tēburu to onaji ryōri o onegai shimasu.

⑧ **I'd like the same.**

わたしも、同じで。

Watashi mo, onaji de.

⑨ **I think I'll order a la carte.** (speaking to yourself)

アラカルトにしようかな……。

Arakaruto ni shiyō ka na . . .

⑩ **Can we order takeout?**

テイク・アウト、できますか?

Teiku-auto, dekimasu ka?

## Questions

MP3
06_03

① **What's in season?**

いま旬のものは、何ですか?

Ima shun no mono wa, nan desu ka?

② **Is this a vegetarian dish?**

これは、ベジタリアン向けですか？

Kore wa, bejitarian-muke desu ka?

③ **Will this be very spicy?**

これ、辛いですか？

Kore, karai desu ka?

④ **What is today's fish?**

きょうの魚料理は何ですか？

Kyō no sakana-ryōri wa nan desu ka?

⑤ **What's in this?**

この料理、中身は何ですか？

Kono ryōri, nakami wa nan desu ka?

⑥ **What is this dish called?**

これは、何というお料理ですか？

Kore wa, nan to iu o-ryōri desu ka?

⑦ **Is it served raw?**

これは、生で食べるものですか？

Kore wa, nama de taberumono desu ka?

⑧ **What size is the portion?**

一人前の量って、どのくらいですか？

Ichinin-mae no ryō tte, dono kurai desu ka?

⑨ **How long will it take to prepare?**

時間はどれくらいかかりますか？

Jikan wa dorekurai kakarimasu ka?

# Concerns and Requests

06_04

① **I can't eat tomatoes, so can you take them out?**

わたし、トマトがダメなんです。
トマト抜きにしてもらえますか？

Watashi, tomato ga dame nan desu.
Tomato-nuki ni shite moraemasu ka?

② **Can you make this dish without salt?**

この料理、塩抜きで作ってもらえませんか？

Kono ryōri, shio-nuki de tsukutte moraemasen ka?

③ **I'm highly allergic to wheat.**

わたし、かなり強い小麦アレルギーがあるんです。

Watashi, kanari tsuyoi komugi-arerugī ga aru n' desu.

④ **I'm scared to try this.**

これ、食べるの、勇気いるなぁ……。

Kore, taberu no, yūki iru nā . . .

⑤ **Is this exactly what I ordered?**

これ、注文した料理にまちがいありませんか？

Kore, chūmon shita ryōri ni machigai arimasen ka?

⑥ **Is our order coming soon?**

料理、まだですか？

Ryōri, mada desu ka?

⑦ **Excuse me . . . I dropped a chopstick . . .**

すみません、箸、落としちゃったんですけど。

Sumimasen, hashi, otoshichatta n' desu kedo.

⑧ **Ma'am . . . could I have another napkin?**

すみません、ナプキン、もう1枚いただけますか？

Sumimasen, napukin, mō ichimai itadakemasu ka?

⑨ **Sir . . . can I change my order?**

すみません、注文を変更しても、いいですか？

Sumimasen, chūmon o henkō shite mo ii desu ka?

Eating Out

# Complaints

MP3
06_05

① **This isn't cooked enough.**

これ、ちゃんと火が通ってませんよ。

Kore, chanto hi ga tōtte 'masen yo.

② **I need a new fork. This one isn't clean.**

フォークが汚れています。取り替えてください。

Fōku ga yogorete imasu. Torikaete kudasai.

③ **Something doesn't taste right.**

何か、おかしな味がするんですけど。

Nanika, okashi na aji ga suru n' desu kedo.

④ **I ordered soup, but it never came.**

スープを頼んだのに、来ませんでした。

Sūpu o tanonda no ni, kimasen deshita.

⑤ **There's *something* in my salad . . .**

サラダに、変なものがはいってます！

Sarada ni, hen na mono ga haitte imasu!

⑥ **I think this wine is corked.**

このワイン、劣化してると思います。

Kono wain, rekka shite 'ru to omoimasu.

⑦ **This is too heavy for me.**

この料理、わたしには脂っこすぎます。

Kono ryōri, watashi ni wa aburakkosugimasu.

⑧ **I'm sorry, but this smells bad.**

すみません、これ、においが変です。

Sumimasen, kore, nioi ga hen desu.

⑨ **This isn't what I ordered.**

これ、注文した料理とちがいます。

Kore, chūmon shita ryōri to chigaimasu.

⑩ **Sorry, but I simply can't eat this.**

申し訳ないけど、これはどうしても食べられません。

Mōshiwakenai kedo, kore wa dōshite mo taberaremasen.

## Compliments

MP3
06_06

① **This is excellent!**

すごく、おいしいです！

Sugoku, oishii desu!

② **This place is a real find.**

この店は、めっけものだね。

Kono mise wa, mekkemono da ne.

③ **What a delicious meal!**

ほんと、おいしかったね！

Honto, oishikatta ne!

④ **This has such a delicate flavor.**

とても繊細な味わいですね。

Totemo sensai na ajiwai desu ne.

⑤ **Can you tell me how you make this?**

これ、どうやって作るんですか？

Kore, dō yatte tsukuru n' desu ka?

⑥ **The service here is superb.**

この店のサービスは、超一流ですね。

Kono mise no sābisu wa, chō-ichiryū desu ne.

⑦ **I'll certainly come here again.**

また、きっと、寄らせてもらいます。

Mata, kitto, yorasete moraimasu.

⑧ **Please give my compliments to the chef.**

シェフに、よろしくお伝えください。

Shefu ni, yoroshiku otsutae kudasai.

⑨ **Do you have a card or pamphlet?**

この店のカードかパンフレット、ありますか？

Kono mise no kādo ka panfuretto, arimasu ka?

**Eating Out**

## Settling the Bill

**MP3**
06_07

① **Check please!**
お会計、お願いします。
O-kaikei, onegai shimasu.

② **Should we pay here or at the register?**
お会計は、ここですか？　レジですか？
O-kaikei wa, koko desu ka? Reji desu ka?

③ **Let me get this.**
ここは、ごちそうさせてください。
Koko wa, gochisō sasete kudasai.

④ **No, it's my turn to get the bill.**
だめだめ、今回はわたしに払わせてください。
Damedame, konkai wa watashi ni harawasete kudasai.

⑤ **Shall we split the bill?**
割り勘にする？
Warikan ni suru?

⑥ **I'm not sure this check is correct.**
この計算、これで合ってますか？
Kono keisan, kore de atte 'masu ka?

⑦ **We didn't order this.**
これは注文しませんでした。
Kore wa chūmon shimasen deshita.

⑧ **Show me an itemized receipt.**

明細書を見せてください。

Meisaisho o misete kudasai.

⑨ **Is this the correct change?**

おつり、これで合ってますか？

Otsuri, kore de atte 'masu ka?

⑩ **May I have a written receipt?**

手書きの領収書をお願いします。

Tegaki no ryōshūsho o onegai shimasu.

**Eating Out**

## Unique Situations

MP3
06_08

① **I have trouble sitting on tatami.**

畳に座るのは、苦手です。

Tatami ni suwaru no wa, nigate desu.

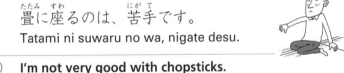

② **I'm not very good with chopsticks.**

お箸は、あまりうまく使えないんです。

O-hashi wa, amari umaku tsukaenai n' desu.

③ **I'm squeamish about raw fish.**

生の魚は、ちょっと、どうも……。

Nama no sakana wa, chotto, dōmo . . .

④ **I can't read anything on this menu.**

このメニュー、読めないんですけど……。

Kono menyū, yomenai n' desu kedo . . .

⑤ **Can you tell me what this says?**

これ、何と書いてあるんですか？

Kore, nan to kaite aru n desu ka?

⑥ **Which one is the ladies' toilet?**

女性用のトイレは、どっちですか？

Josei-yō no toire wa, dotchi desu ka?

⑦ **Even Japanese don't usually eat this, do they?**

日本人でも、こういうものは、
あまり食べないんでしょう？

Nihonjin demo, kō iu mono wa,
amari tabenai n' deshō?

⑧ **Where are the napkins?**

ナプキンは、ありませんか？

Napukin wa, arimasen ka?

⑨ **Pardon me, but what the heck *is* this?**

悪いけど、これって、いったい何ですか？

Warui kedo, kore tte, ittai nan desu ka?

⑩ **I spilled my drink, so could you bring some towels?**

こぼしちゃったので、おしぼりをもらえますか？

Koboshichatta no de, oshibori o moraemasu ka?

⑪ **This is something to write home about!**

これは、ぜひ、うちの家族に教えてあげなくちゃ！

Kore wa, zehi, uchi no kazoku ni oshiete agenakucha!

# Hanging with Friends

## Invitations

07_01

① **Want to grab a bite?**

ごはん、食べに行かない？

Gohan, tabe ni ikanai?

② **Let's go get a beer.**

ビール、一杯どう？

Bīru, ippai dō?

③ **If you're free Friday, let's do lunch.**

金曜日、あいてる？　よかったら、ランチしない？

Kin'yōbi, aiteru? Yokattara, ranchi shinai?

④ **We're having a barbecue. Would you like to come?**

うちでバーベキューするんですけど、

いらっしゃいませんか？

Uchi de bābekyū suru n' desu kedo,
irasshaimasen ka?

⑤ **Can you join us for a potluck dinner?**

料理を持ち寄って夕食会をするけど、来ない？

Ryōri o mochiyotte yūshokukai o suru kedo, konai?

⑥ **Let's do coffee sometime.**

こんど、お茶しない？ (lit., Tea sometime?)

Kondo, ocha shinai?

⑦ **Thanks. Definitely. Count me in.**

ありがとう。もちろん出席です。

数に入れといて！

Arigatō. Mochiron shusseki desu.

Kazu ni iretoite!

⑧ **We'd love to come.**

よろこんで、おじゃまします。

Yorokonde, ojama shimasu.

⑨ **Are you kidding? Of course!**

もちろん、行くにきまってるじゃん！

Mochiron, iku ni kimatte 'ru jan!

⑩ **Sorry, but I'm booked then.**

ごめんなさい、その日は予定があるんです。

Gomen nasai, sono hi wa yotei ga aru n' desu.

⑪ **I'm afraid Thursday is no good.**

木曜日は、ダメそうです。

Mokuyōbi wa, damesō desu.

⑫ **Can I take a rain check?**

またこんど、誘ってね。

Mata kondo, sasotte ne.

# Details

MP3
07_02

① **It's BYOB.**

ドリンクは、各自持参で。

Dorinku wa, kakuji-jisan de.

② **I hope you like Italian.**

イタリアン、だいじょうぶだよね？

Itarian, daijōbu da yo ne?

③ **RSVP as soon as you can.**

なるべく早くお返事ください。

Narubeku hayaku o-henji kudasai.

④ **What should I bring?**

何を持っていきましょうか？

Nani o motte ikimashō ka?

⑤ **Just bring yourself.**

手ぶらで来てね。

Tebura de kite ne.

⑥ **Is anyone I know coming?**

だれか、わたしの知ってる人、来ますか？

Dareka, watashi no shitte 'ru hito, kimasu ka?

⑦ **Lots of people are coming.**

たくさんの人が来てくれる予定です。

Takusan no hito ga kite kureru yotei desu.

Hanging with Friends

⑧ **I can't drink alcohol . . .**

わたし、お酒、飲めないんです……。

Watashi, o-sake, nomenai n' desu . . .

---

# When the Party Starts

**MP3**

**07_03**

① **Please come in!**

どうぞ、おはいりください！

Dōzo, ohairi kudasai!

---

② **What a lovely gift! You shouldn't have!**

わぁ、すてきなプレゼント！

気をつかわなくて、よかったのに。

Wā, suteki na purezento!

Ki o tsukawanakute yokatta no ni.

---

③ **I'm so glad you could make it.**

ようこそ、お越しくださいました。

Yōkoso, okoshi kudasaimashita.

---

④ **Make yourself at home.**

どうぞ、おくつろぎください。

Dōzo, okutsurogi kudasai.

---

⑤ **Can I get you something to drink?**

ドリンク、何がいいですか？

Dorinku, nani ga ii desu ka?

# Table Talk

07_04

① **Come sit here with me.**

こっちにおいでよ！

Kotchi ni oide yo!

② **Please begin!**

どうぞ、始めてください。

Dōzo, hajimete kudasai.

③ **Could you pass the wine please?**

ワイン、回していただけますか？

Wain, mawashite itadakemasu ka?

④ **I'd like to toast our friends.**

友だちに乾杯！

Tomodachi ni kampai!

⑤ **Would you like a second helping?**

お代わりは、いかがですか？

Okawari wa, ikaga desu ka?

⑥ **What can I get you?**

何か、取りましょうか？

Nanika, torimashō ka?

⑦ **This is how you eat it.**

こうやって食べてみて……。

Kōyatte tabete mite . . .

Hanging with Friends

⑧ **Won't you take this last bit?**

あと一口、いかがですか？

Ato hitokuchi, ikaga desu ka?

⑨ **Excuse me for just a minute.**

ちょっと失礼します。

Chotto shitsurei shimasu.

⑩ **Just leave everything. I'll get it later.**

そのまま置いといて。あとでやるから。

Sonomama oitoite. Atode yaru kara.

⑪ **We still have dessert and coffee.**

このあと、まだデザートとコーヒーがあります。

Kono ato, mada dezāto to kōhī ga arimasu.

⑫ **Can you stay for a cognac?**

もう少しゆっくりして、コニャックでも、

いかがですか？

Mō sukoshi yukkuri shite, konyakku demo
ikaga desu ka?

# Ordering Delivery

MP3

07_05

① **The address is . . .**

住所は……。

Jūsho wa . . .

② **I'd like three large pepperoni pizzas.**

ラージサイズのペパロニ・ピザを3枚、
お願いします。

Rāji-saizu no peparoni piza o sammai,
onegai shimasu.

③ **I have a discount coupon.**

割引券があるんですけど。

Waribikiken ga aru n' desu kedo.

④ **Do you think that's enough for four adults?**

これ、大人4人に十分な量ですか？

Kore, otona yonin ni jūbun na ryō desu ka?

⑤ **How long will it take to get here?**

何分くらい、かかりますか？

Nampun kurai, kakarimasu ka?

# How's the Food?

07_06

① **I made this from scratch.**

これ、わたしの手作りです。

Kore, watashi no tezukuri desu.

② **Have you ever tried this?**

これ、召し上がったこと、ありますか？

Kore, meshiagatta koto, arimasu ka?

③ **This is the first time I've ever made this.**

F この料理、初めて作ったの。

Kono ryōri, hajimete tsukutta no.

M この料理、初めて作ったんだ。

Kono ryōri, hajimete tsukutta n' da.

④ **This is amazing! How did you make it?**

おいしいですね！　どうやって作ったんですか？

Oishii desu ne! Dō yatte tsukutta n' desu ka?

⑤ **It's an old family recipe.**

我が家に代々伝わるレシピなんです。

Wagaya ni daidai tsutawaru reshipi nan desu.

⑥ **I'm so glad that you like it.**

喜んでいただけて、すごくうれしいです。

Yorokonde itadakete, sugoku ureshii desu.

# Lay It Out on the Table

MP3

07_07

① **Can I tell you a secret?**

ないしょの話、聞いてくれる？

Naisho no hanashi, kiite kureru?

② **If you want my honest opinion . . .**

率直に言わせてもらうなら……。

Sotchoku ni iwasete morau nara . . .

③ **Frankly, just between you and me . . .**

ここだけの話<ruby>話<rt>はなし</rt></ruby>だけど……。

Koko dake no hanashi da kedo . . .

④ **I've been meaning to ask you . . .**

ずっと<ruby>聞<rt>き</rt></ruby>いてみたかったんだけど……。

Zutto kiite mitakatta n' da kedo . . .

⑤ **This is a pretty personal question, but . . .**

<ruby>立<rt>た</rt></ruby>ち<ruby>入<rt>い</rt></ruby>ったことを<ruby>伺<rt>うかが</rt></ruby>いますが……。

Tachiitta koto o ukagaimasu ga . . .

⑥ **This has been bothering me for ages.**

M ずっと<ruby>前<rt>まえ</rt></ruby>から<ruby>気<rt>き</rt></ruby>になってたんだ。

Zutto mae kara ki ni natte 'ta n' da.

F ずっと<ruby>前<rt>まえ</rt></ruby>から、<ruby>気<rt>き</rt></ruby>になってたの。

Zutto mae kara ki ni natte 'ta no.

⑦ **Don't let this get out, okay?**

この<ruby>話<rt>はなし</rt></ruby>、ほかの<ruby>人<rt>ひと</rt></ruby>には<ruby>言<rt>い</rt></ruby>わないでね。

Kono hanashi, hoka no hito ni wa iwanaide ne.

⑧ **Don't take this the wrong way, but . . .**

<ruby>誤解<rt>ごかい</rt></ruby>しないでほしいんだけど……。

Gokai shinaide hoshii n' da kedo . . .

⑨ **So, what's the real story on that?**

で、<ruby>本当<rt>ほんとう</rt></ruby>のところは、どうなの？

De, hontō no tokoro wa dō na no?

⑩ **Let me level with you.**
ぶっちゃけて話すよ。
Butchakete hanasu yo.

⑪ **This isn't easy to talk about, but . . .**
ちょっと話しにくいんだけど……。
Chotto hanashinikui n' da kedo . . .

⑫ **I completely hear what you're saying.**
うん、わかる、わかるよ……。
Un, wakaru, wakaru yo . . .

## Parting and Postmortem

MP3
07_08

① **The night is still young!**
まだまだ、夜はこれからですよ！
Madamada, yoru wa kore kara desu yo!

② **Is anyone up for barhopping?**
だれか、これからハシゴしたい人〜？
Dareka, kore kara hashigo shitai hitō?

③ **I have to get going.**
そろそろ失礼しないと……。
Sorosoro shitsurei shinai to . . .

④ **Do you really have to go?**
どうしても帰らなくちゃだめ？
Dōshitemo kaeranakucha dame?

⑤ **Tomorrow comes pretty early . . .**

夜もだいぶ更けてきたし……。

Yoru mo daibu fukete kita shi . . .

⑥ **This was so much fun.**

ほんと、おもしろかったね。

Honto, omoshirokatta ne.

⑦ **We need to call a cab.**

タクシー呼ばなくちゃ。

Takushī yobanakucha.

⑧ **Can you find your way back?**

帰り道、わかる？

Kaerimichi, wakaru?

⑨ **Please come again soon.**

ぜひ、また来てね！

Zehi, mata kite ne!

⑩ **We had such a great time!**

楽しかったね！

Tanoshikatta ne!

⑪ **Let's do that again soon.**

また、近々やりましょう。

Mata, chikajika yarimashō.

⑫ **Ugh, I'm wasted!**

あ〜、酔っぱらった！

Ā, yopparatta!

⑬ **I'm going to be so hungover tomorrow.**

あしたは、ひどい二日酔いになりそう。

Ashita wa, hidoi futsukayoi ni narisō.

---

⑭ **Hair of the dog that bit you?**

M おっ、迎え酒？

　　O, mukaezake?

F あら、迎え酒？

　　Ara, mukaezake?

---

### Raising a Glass

Japanese love to get together to knock back some glasses with friends. Because homes are often fairly small, and tucked right up next to the neighbors' place, most social drinking happens outside the home, at company events, restaurants, bars, or small establishments serving casual traditional Japanese food, called **izakaya**.

Tip One: It's not polite to pour for yourself until you have filled everyone else's glass, and even then it's better to put the bottle down and let someone else have the honor of pouring for you. By all means, lift your glass when someone pours for you, or you will seem ever so slightly condescending to your buddies.

Tip Two: Getting toasted allows for everyone to let down inhibitions, and you will see an entirely different side to many Japanese under these circumstances. In Japanese society, drinking allows everyone leniency, and while you may hear wild gossip or passionate diatribes at the company party, rarely are people held responsible the next day for minor indiscretions and revelations while drunk.

## Physique

MP3

08_01

① **He's about my height, and skinny.**

彼はわたしと同じくらいの身長で、やせています。

Kare wa watashi to onaji kurai no shinchō de, yasete imasu.

② **She's squat and slightly plump.**

彼女、ずんぐりむっくりって感じだね。

Kanojo, zunguri-mukkuri tte kanji da ne.

③ **He's tall, dark, and handsome.**

F 彼、背が高くて、日焼けしてて、

ハンサムなの。

Kare, se ga takakute, hiyake shite 'te,
hansamu na no.

M あいつは背が高くて、日焼けしてて、

ハンサムだよ。

Aitsu wa se ga takakute, hiyake shite 'te,
hansamu da yo.

④ **He's short and stocky.**

彼は、背が低くて、がっしりした体格です。

Kare wa, se ga hikukute, gasshiri shita taikaku desu.

⑤ **He's athletic and muscular.**

F 彼、スポーツマンだけあって、

いいカラダしてるわよ。

Kare, supōtsuman dake atte,
ii karada shite 'ru wa yo.

M あいつはスポーツマンだけあって、

いいカラダしてるよ。

Aitsu wa supōtsuman dake atte,
ii karada shite 'ru yo.

⑥ **He's built like a beanpole.**
彼はのっぽだよ。
Kare wa noppo da yo.

⑦ **She's tiny, and light as a feather.**
彼女、すごく小柄で、きゃしゃなんだ。
Kanojo, sugoku kogarade, kyasha nan da.

⑧ **She's just skin and bones.**
彼女、ガリガリだね。
Kanojo, garigari da ne.

⑨ **He really needs to hit the gym.**
あの人、もうちょっと
運動したほうがいいよね。
Ano hito, mō chotto,
undō shita hō ga ii yo ne.

# Hair

**MP3**
08_02

① **His hair is receding.**

彼、生えぎわが後退しはじめてるね。

Kare, haegiwa ga kōtai shihajimete 'ru ne.

② **Did you get a new haircut?**

ヘア・スタイル、変えた？

Heasutairu, kaeta?

③ **Believe it or not, that's her natural hair color.**

信じらんないかもしれないけど、
あの髪の色は生まれつきなんだよ。

Shinjirannai ka mo shirenai kedo,
ano kami no iro wa umaretsuki nan da yo.

④ **She tends to over-style her hair.**

彼女、ちょっと、髪、いじりすぎだよね。

Kanojo, chotto, kami ijirisugi da yo ne.

⑤ **She usually wears her hair loose.**

彼女、ふだんは髪を結ばずに下ろしてるよ。

Kanojo, fudan wa kami o musubazu ni oroshite 'ru yo.

⑥ **She looks good with short hair.**

あの人、ショート・カットが似合うね。

Ano hito, shōto-katto ga niau ne.

⑦ **He's always clean-shaven.**

彼は、いつも、ひげをきちんと剃っていますよ。

Kare wa, itsumo, hige o kichinto sotte imasu yo.

⑧ **He's got sideburns and a goatee.**

その人は、もみあげとやぎひげを
伸ばしています。

Sono hito wa, momiage to yagihige o
nobashite imasu.

⑨ **He has a trim beard and moustache.**

彼は、あごひげと口ひげをきちんと
手入れしています。

Kare wa, agohige to kuchihige o kichinto
te-ire shite imasu.

# Ears, Eyes, Nose, and Lips

08_03

① **His ears really stick out.**

あの人の耳、すごく目立つね。

Ano hito no mimi, sugku medatsu ne.

② **Does she have pierced ears?**

あの人、耳にピアスしてたっけ？

Ano hito, mimi ni piasu shite 'ta kke?

③ **She has beautiful green eyes.**

彼女、すてきなグリーンの目をしてるんだよ。

Kanojo, suteki na gurīn no me o shite 'ru n' da yo.

④ **He has beady little eyes.**

彼は、きらきら輝く小さな目をしてるんです。

Kare wa, kirakira kagayaku chiisa na me o shite 'ru n' desu.

⑤ **She has a very distinctive profile.**

彼女の横顔は、すごく
特徴的ですよ。

Kanojo no yokogao wa, sugoku
tokuchōteki desu yo.

⑥ **He has a pretty wide nose.**

彼は、立派な鼻をしてるんですよ。

Kare wa, rippa na hana o shite 'ru n' desu yo.

⑦ **She has full lips and beautiful black hair.**

彼女、唇がふっくらしてて、
黒い髪がつやつやなんです。

Kanojo, kuchibiru ga fukkura shite 'te,
kuroi kami ga tsuyatsuya nan desu.

Talking about People

# Limbs

① **She's bowlegged.**
あの人、〇脚だよ。
Ano hito, ōkyaku da yo.

② **He has really long legs.**
彼、足が長いんだ。
Kare, ashi ga nagai n' da.

③ **She can't walk without a crutch.**
彼女は、松葉づえなしでは歩けません。
Kanojo wa, matsubazue nashi de wa arukemasen.

④ **He's in a wheelchair.**
彼は、車椅子の生活です。
Kare wa, kurumaisu no seikatsu desu.

⑤ **He has broad shoulders and strong arms.**
F 彼って、肩幅が広いし、腕もたくましいの。
Kare tte, katahaba ga hiroi shi, ude mo takumashii no.

⑥ **You really have tiny hands.**
ずいぶん小さな手をしてるんだね。
Zuibun chiisa na te o shite 'ru n' da ne.

⑦ **He's sort of gangly.**
彼は、背が高くて、ひょろひょろです。
Kare wa, se ga takakute, hyorohyoro desu.

# Chest, Belly, and Buns

08_05

① **I'm looking for a guy with a six-pack.**

F わたし、
腹筋の割れた男がいいな……。

Watashi,
fukkin no wareta otoko ga ii na . . .

---

② **She has great boobs.**

M 彼女、巨乳なんだ。

Kanojo, kyonyū nan da.

---

③ **I like a man with love handles.**

F わたしは、ウエストのはみ肉がつかめる
くらいの人、好きよ。

Watashi wa, uesuto no haminiku ga tsukameru
kurai no hito, suki yo.

---

④ **He has a potbelly.**

あの人、たいこ腹だね。

Ano hito, taikobara da ne.

---

⑤ **He's got a cute butt.**

F 彼、かわいいお尻してるの。

Kare, kawaii oshiri shite 'ru no.

⑥ **I like women with curves.**

M おれは、グラマーが好<sup>す</sup>きだな。

Ore wa, guramā ga suki da na.

# Overall Looks

**08_06**

① **He's a total hunk.**

F いい男<sup>おとこ</sup>ねえ！

Ii otoko nē!

② **She's a hottie.**

M 彼女<sup>かのじょ</sup>、超<sup>ちょう</sup>セクシーだな！

Kanojo, chō-sekushī da na!

③ **Talk about a girlie man!**

F なんて女々<sup>めめ</sup>しい男<sup>おとこ</sup>なの！

Nante memeshii otoko na no!

M なんだよ、あいつ、女々<sup>めめ</sup>しいな！

Nan da yo, aitsu, memeshii na!

④ **He's kind of a slob.**

あの人<sup>ひと</sup>、ちょっと不潔<sup>ふけつ</sup>っぽいね。

Ano hito, chotto fuketsu-ppoi ne.

⑤ **She really stands out in a crowd.**

あの娘<sup>こ</sup>、ほんと、目立<sup>めだ</sup>つよね。

Ano ko, honto, medatsu yo ne.

⑥ **She's in great shape.**
彼女は、スタイル抜群だよ。
Kanojo wa, sutairu batsugun da yo.

⑦ **He has really let himself go.**
あの人、身なりを全然かまわなくなったね。
Ano hito, minari o zenzen kamawanaku natta ne.

⑧ **He looks like your typical office grunt.**
あの人、見るからにヒラ社員っぽいよね。
Ano hito, mirukarani hirashain-ppoi yo ne

## Personality: Good Traits

MP3
08_07

① **You won't find a nicer person.**
あんないい人、いませんよ。
Anna ii hito, imasen yo.

② **He really listens.**
あの人なら、じっくり話を聞いてくれるよ。
Ano hito nara, jikkuri hanashi o kiite kureru yo.

③ **She's trustworthy.**
彼女は信頼できる人だよ。
Kanojo wa shinrai dekiru hito da yo.

④ **They're always relaxed and easygoing.**
あの人たちなら、気が置けないね。
Ano hitotachi nara, ki ga okenai ne.

Talking about People

126

⑤ **He's got a great sense of humor.**

M あいつ、ユーモアのセンス、抜群だよ。

Aitsu, yūmoa no sensu, batsugun da yo.

F 彼、ユーモアのセンスが抜群なの。

Kare, yūmoa no sensu ga batsugun na no.

⑥ **She'll back you up completely.**

彼女は、とことん後ろ盾になってくれる人だと
思うよ。

Kanojo wa, tokoton ushirodate ni natte kureru hito da to
omou yo.

⑦ **He's supportive and genuinely kind.**

彼は世話好きで、とってもいい人ですよ。

Kare wa sewazukide, tottemo ii hito desu yo.

⑧ **She thinks outside the box.**

彼女は、型にはまらない考え方のできる人です。

Kanojo wa, kata ni hamaranai kangaekata no dekiru hito desu.

⑨ **She's so smart.**

彼女はすごく頭が切れるんだよ。

Kanojo wa sugoku atama ga kireru n' da yo.

⑩ **He's a hard worker.**

あの人は、働き者です。

Ano hito wa, hatarakimono desu.

⑪ **She's very diligent.**

彼女は、努力家ですよ。

Kanojo wa, doryokuka desu yo.

⑫ **He's got balls of steel.**

彼は、肝っ玉がすわっている。

Kare wa, kimottama ga suwatte iru.

⑬ **She's shy but sweet.**

彼女、恥ずかしがりだけど、優しい人だよ。

Kanojo, hazukashigari da kedo, yasashii hito da yo.

⑭ **She's an incredibly generous person.**

彼女は、とっても寛大な人ですよ。

Kanojo wa, tottemo kandai na hito desu yo.

⑮ **He really gets stuff done.**

あの人は実行力があるね。

Ano hito wa jikkōryoku ga aru ne.

⑯ **She's fun to be with.**

彼女、一緒にいて楽しい人だよ。

Kanojo, issho ni ite tanoshii hito da yo.

⑰ **She's friendly and outgoing.**

彼女は、気さくで社交的な性格です。

Kanojo wa, kisaku de shakōteki na seikaku desu.

⑱ **When he talks, people listen.**

あの人の言葉には、力がありますよ。

Ano hito no kotoba ni wa, chikara ga arimasu yo.

Talking about People

# Personality: Bad Traits

MP3

08_08

① **He's depressing to be around.**

あの人のそばにいると、ゆううつになる……。

Ano hito no soba ni iru to, yūutsu ni naru . . .

② **She's always complaining about stuff.**

彼女って、愚痴ばっかり言ってるよね。

Kanojo tte, guchi bakkari itteru yo ne.

③ **You can't believe a word she says.**

あの人の言うことは、何ひとつ信用できないよ。

Ano hito no iu koto wa, nanihitotsu shin'yō dekinai yo.

④ **He'll talk behind your back.**

M あいつは、陰で人の悪口を言うような
男なんだよ。

Aitsu wa, kage de hito no waruguchi o iu yō na
otoko nan da yo.

F 彼、陰で人の悪口を言うような
男なのよ。

Kare, kage de hito no waruguchi o iu yō na
otoko na no yo.

⑤ **He's a total pain in the ass.**

ほんと、腹の立つ男だね！

Honto, hara no tatsu otoko da ne!

⑥ **He's full of himself.**

あの人は、うぬぼれ屋ですよ。

Ano hito wa, unuboreya desu yo.

⑦ **He's a liar.**

あの男は、嘘つきだよ。

Ano otoko wa, usotsuki da yo.

⑧ **She can be really bitchy.**

彼女、じつにいやな女になるときが

あるんだよね。

Kanojo, jitsuni iya na onna ni naru toki ga
aru n' da yo ne.

⑨ **He's kind of a pervert.**

彼、ちょっと変態の気があるね。

Kare, chotto hentai no ke ga aru ne.

⑩ **She lives for gossip.**

彼女は、他人のゴシップが生きがいなんだ。

Kanojo wa, tanin no goshippu ga ikigai nan da.

⑪ **He's arrogant and short-tempered.**

あの人はごう慢で、すぐに怒りだすんです。

Ano hito wa gōman de, sugu ni okoridasu n' desu.

⑫ **He thinks of no one but himself.**

あの人は、自分のことしか頭にないんだよ。

Ano hito wa, jibun no koto shika atama ni nai n' da yo.

Talking about People

⑬　**He's a control freak.**

あの人は、何でも自分で仕切らないと
気がすまないんです。

Ano hito wa, nandemo jibun de shikiranai to
ki ga sumanai n' desu.

⑭　**She's extremely selfish.**

彼女、めちゃくちゃ自己チューだよ。

Kanojo, mechakucha jikochū da yo.

⑮　**He's a complete goof-off.**

F　彼って、ほんと、いいかげんな男だよね。

Kare tte, honto, iikagen na otoko da yo ne.

M　あいつ、ほんと、いいかげんなヤツだよな。

Aitsu, honto, iikagen na yatsu da yo na.

⑯　**He's a pest.**

M　あれは、うっとうしい男だな。

Are wa, uttōshii otoko da na.

F　あの人、うっとうしいよね。

Ano hito, uttōshii yo ne.

⑰　**She can be wishy-washy.**

彼女、優柔不断なところがあるんだよね。

Kanojo, yūjū-fudan na tokoro ga aru n' da yo ne.

# Lifestyle

MP3

08_09

① **He's rich.**

あの人は、お金持ちですよ。

Ano hito wa, o-kanemochi desu yo.

② **They're dirt poor.**

あの人たち、無一文なんです。

Ano hitotachi, muichimon nan desu.

③ **She's got the best job in the world.**

彼女、すごくいい仕事に恵まれてるよ。

Kanojo, sugoku ii shigoto ni megumarete 'ru yo.

④ **He throws away his money.**

F 彼、お金を湯水のように使うのよ。

Kare, o-kane o yumizu no yō ni tsukau no yo.

M あいつ、カネを湯水のように使うんだ。

Aitsu, kane o yumizu no yō ni tsukau n' da.

⑤ **They worry about keeping up with the Joneses.**

あの人たち、となり近所と
張り合うことばっかり考えてるんだから。

Ano hitotachi, tonarikinjo to
hariau koto bakkari kangaete 'ru n' da kara.

Talking about People

⑥ **He lives like a king.**

あの人は、王様のような暮らしをしてますよ。

Ano hito wa, ōsama no yō na kurashi o shite 'masu yo.

---

⑦ **They don't get out much.**

あの人たちは、付き合いが広いほうでは

ありません。

Ano hitotachi wa, tsukiai ga hiroi hō de wa

arimasen.

---

⑧ **He's a party animal.**

彼は、パーティーにうつつを抜かしてる。

Kare wa, pātī ni utsutsu o nukashite 'ru.

---

⑨ **They're comfortably retired.**

彼らは引退して、

悠々自適の暮らしをしています。

Karera wa intai shite,

yūyūjiteki no kurashi o shite imasu.

# Social Interaction

## Initiating a Chat

09_01

① **Can you believe this weather?**

すごい天気ですね。

Sugoi tenki desu ne.

② **Long time no see!**

ひさしぶり！

Hisashiburi!

③ **How was your weekend?**

週末、どうだった？

Shūmatsu, dō datta?

④ **Where have you been lately?**

最近、どうしてた？

Saikin, dō shite 'ta?

⑤ **How did it go yesterday?**

どうだった、きのう？

Dō datta, kinō?

⑥ **So what's up with you?**

どう、調子は？

Dō, chōshi wa?

⑦ **Hey, did you hear the latest?**

ねえ、聞いた？

Nē, kiita?

---

⑧ **Hey, what's with the new look?**

どうしちゃったの、きょうは？

Dōshichatta no, kyō wa?

---

⑨ **I've got great news.**

すごいニュースがあるんだ！

Sugoi nyūsu ga aru n' da!

---

⑩ **Let's go get a cup of coffee.**

コーヒー、飲みにいかない？

Kōhī, nomi ni ikanai?

---

# Getting and Giving Opinions

09_02

---

① **I need to pick your brain on this.**

この件について、知恵を貸してもらえないかな……。

Kono ken ni tsuite, chie o kashite moraenai ka na . . .

---

② **I want your thoughts on the meeting.**

例の会議について、考えを聞かせてください。

Rei no kaigi ni tsuite, kangae o kikasete kudasai.

---

③ **How does that strike you?**

どう思う？

Dō omou?

④ **What do you make of all this?**
こういう話なんだけど、どう思う？
Kō iu hanashi nan da kedo, dō omou?

⑤ **Here's my two-cents' worth.**
出過ぎたことを言うようですが……。
Desugita koto o iu yō desu ga . . .

⑥ **Here's how I see it.**
わたしは、こう思うんです。
Watashi wa, kō omou n' desu.

⑦ **This is just my personal opinion.**
ま、単に、わたしの個人的な考えですけどね。
Ma, tanni, watashi no kojinteki na kangae desu kedo ne.

⑧ **I'm not sure what to say.**
何と言えばいいのか、わかりません。
Nanto ieba ii no ka, wakarimasen.

⑨ **I'm not the best person to ask.**
ほかの人に聞いたほうがいいかも。
Hoka no hito ni kiita hō ga ii kamo.

# Agreeing and Disagreeing

MP3
09_03

① **That seems perfectly reasonable.**
それは、もっともな話だと思うよ。
Sore wa, mottomo na hanashi da to omou yo.

② **I'm in total agreement.**

そうですね、百パーセント同感です。

Sō desu ne, hyakupāsento dōkan desu.

③ **Sounds like a plan.**

いい考えだね。

Ii kangae da ne.

④ **I'm with you on that.**

その点については、わたしも同じ意見です。

Sono ten ni tsuite wa, watashi mo onaji iken desu.

⑤ **You've made some good points.**

鋭い指摘ですね。

Surudoi shiteki desu ne.

⑥ **That's not going to work.**

そんなの、うまくいくわけないよ。

Sonna no, umaku iku wake nai yo.

⑦ **I have some hesitations about that.**

諸手を上げて賛成、とはいきませんね。

Morote o agete sansei, to wa ikimasen ne.

⑧ **I strongly disagree.**

大いに異議ありです。

Ōi ni igi ari desu.

⑨ **I don't think that's quite right.**

そうとも言い切れないんじゃないかな……。

Sō tomo iikirenai n' ja nai ka na . . .

# Making Suggestions

**MP3**

09_04

① **If I were you . . .**

わたしだったら……。

Watashi dattara . . .

② **Here's an idea . . .**

こういう考えもありますよ……。

Kō iu kangae mo arimasu yo . . .

③ **You'd better be careful.**

気を付けたほうがいいですよ。

Ki o tsuketa hō ga ii desu yo.

④ **You might want to rethink that.**

考えなおしたほうが、いいかも……。

Kangaenaoshita hō ga, ii ka mo . . .

⑤ **Maybe we should forget it.**

やめたほうが、よさそうだね。

Yameta hō ga, yosasō da ne.

⑥ **You should give it a try.**

いちど、やってみるべきだよ。

Ichido, yatte miru beki da yo.

⑦ **Why not give him a chance?**

彼にやらせてみれば？

Kare ni yarasete mireba?

⑧ **Better start over from scratch.**

一からやり直したほうがいいね。

Ichi kara yarinaoshita hō ga ii ne.

---

# Hesitating and Resisting

MP3
09_05

① **I don't know if I really want to do that.**

うーん、迷うなぁ……。

Ūn, mayou nā . . .

② **I'm reluctant to do that.**

気が進まないなぁ。

Ki ga susumanai nā.

---

③ **I wish I could say yes, but I'm not sure yet.**

「イエス」と言いたいところですが、

まだわかりません。

"Iesu" to iitai tokoro desu ga,
mada wakarimasen.

---

④ **It's not something I want to jump into.**

喜び勇んでやる気には、なれません。

Yorokobi-isande yaru ki ni wa, naremasen.

---

⑤ **This makes me nervous.**

自信ないなぁ。

Jishin nai nā.

⑥ **Why should I?**

なんで？　やだよ。

Nande? Ya da yo.

⑦ **I don't think so!**

それ、ありえないから！

Sore, arienai kara!

⑧ **No way!**

冗談じゃない！

Jōdan ja nai!

# Words of Encouragement

MP3
09_06

① **Go for it.**

がんばれ！

Gambare!

② **Give it your best shot.**

やれるだけ、やってみなよ。

Yareru dake, yatte mina yo.

③ **You'll do just fine!**

だいじょうぶ、うまくいくよ！

Daijōbu, umaku iku yo!

④ **You're doing a great job.**

よくやってるじゃないですか。

Yoku yatte 'ru ja nai desu ka.

⑤ **Don't let the bastards get you down.**

F あんな人たちの言うことなんか、
気にしなくていいよ。
Anna hitotachi no iu koto nanka,
ki ni shinakute ii yo.

M あんなやつらの言うことなんか、
気にしなくていいよ。
Anna yatsura no iu koto nanka,
ki ni shinakute ii yo.

⑥ **Come on, you can do it!**

M できるよ、がんばれ！
Dekiru yo, gambare!

F できるよ、がんばって！
Dekiru yo, gambatte!

⑦ **Don't hesitate.**
思いきって、やってごらんよ。
Omoikitte yatte goran yo.

⑧ **You're on the right track.**
そう、その調子！
Sō, sono chōshi!

⑨ **Don't give up.**
あきらめないで。
Akiramenaide.

⑩ **You won't regret it.**

だいじょうぶ、うまくいくって！

Daijōbu, umaku iku tte!

⑪ **We're all behind you!**

F わたしたちが、付いてるよ！

Watashitachi ga tsuite 'ru yo!

M おれたちが付いてるぞ！

Oretachi ga tsuite 'ru zo!

⑫ **Just do it!**

やるしかないよ！

Yaru shika nai yo!

# Getting Things Straight

MP3
09_07

① **Is that a fact?**

それは事実ですか？

Sore wa jijitsu desu ka?

② **Is that really what you said?**

本当に、そう言ったの？

Hontō ni, sō itta no?

③ **Did you mean that?**

本気でおっしゃったのですか？

Honki de osshatta no desu ka?

④ **Let me get this straight . . .**

つまり、こういうことですね？

Tsumari, kō iu koto desu ne?

⑤ **Can you repeat what you just said?**

いまの話、もういちど言ってもらえませんか？

Ima no hanashi, mō ichido itte moraemasen ka?

⑥ **Are you sure that's right?**

ほんとに？　まちがいない？

Honto ni? Machigainai?

⑦ **Run that by me again.**

もういちど言ってみて。

Mō ichido itte mite.

⑧ **Did I miss something?**

え？　聞いてないよ〜。

E? Kiite nai yō.

⑨ **I think you know what I'm saying.**

わたしが言いたいこと、わかってますよね。

Watashi ga iitai koto, wakatte 'masu yo ne.

⑩ **I think you misunderstood me.**

それは誤解だと思います。

Sore wa gokai da to omoimasu.

⑪ **That's not what I meant at all.**

そうじゃない、全然ちがうよ。

Sō ja nai, zenzen chigau yo.

⑫ **What I meant was . . .**

言いたかったのは、こういうことです。

Iitakatta no wa, kō iu koto desu.

⑬ **I never said that!**

そんなこと、言ってませんよ！

Sonna koto, itte 'masen yo!

⑭ **I'm just being honest.**

正直に言っただけです。

Shōjiki ni itta dake desu.

# Equivocating, Deliberating, and Stonewalling

09_08

① **I'm really not sure.**

さぁ、どうかなぁ……。

Sā, dō ka nā . . .

② **That's still up in the air.**

それは、まだ決まってないよ。

Sore wa, mada kimatte 'nai yo.

③ **Maybe yes, and maybe no.**

そうかもしれないし、そうじゃないかもしれない。

Sō ka mo shirenai shi, sō ja nai ka mo shirenai.

④ **I'll consider it and get back to you.**

検討して、のちほどお返事します。

Kentō shite, nochihodo o-henji shimasu.

**⑤   Let me think about it a bit first.**

とりあえず、少し考えさせてください。

Toriaezu, sukoshi kangaesasete kudasai.

---

**⑥   That's not our problem.**

それは、こちらには関係ないことです。

Sore wa, kochira ni wa kankei nai koto desu.

---

**⑦   That was not part of the agreement.**

その点については、合意してませんよ。

Sono ten ni tsuite wa, gōi shite 'masen yo.

---

**⑧   I did the best I could for you.**

あなたに良かれと思って、最善を尽くしたんです。

Anata ni yokare to omotte, saizen o tsukushita n' desu.

---

**⑨   I'd rather not talk about it.**

そのことについては、話したくありません。

Sono koto ni tsuite wa, hanashitaku arimasen.

---

# Taking and Relinquishing Control

09_09

**①   I'll handle this.**

ここは、まかせてください。

Koko wa, makasete kudasai.

---

**②   Let me take care of it from here.**

ここから先は、わたしが引き取りましょう。

Koko kara saki wa, watashi ga hikitorimashō.

③ **Will you back me up on that?**
あの件、後押ししてくれる？
Ano ken, atooshi shite kureru?

④ **Can you take this on yourself?**
これ、頼まれてくれる？
Kore, tanomarete kureru?

⑤ **Let me help you out this time.**
今回は、手伝ってあげるよ。
Konkai wa, tetsudatte ageru yo.

⑥ **You're on your own from here on out.**
ここから先は、自分でやってごらん。
Koko kara saki wa, jibun de yatte goran.

⑦ **That's *your* problem now.**
それは、おたくの問題でしょう？
Sore wa, otaku no mondai deshō?

⑧ **I wash my hands of this business.**
この件からは、手を引かせてもらいます。
Kono ken kara wa, te o hikasete moraimasu.

⑨ **The ball's in your court.**
こんどは、そっちの番だよ。
Kondo wa, sotchi no ban da yo.

# Cooling and Consoling

MP3
09_10

① **Hey, take it easy.**

まあまあ、おちついて。

Māmā, ochitsuite.

② **Don't overdo it.**

ほどほどに、しといたら？

Hodohodo ni, shitoitara?

③ **Don't sweat it so much.**

そんなに焦ることないよ。

Sonna ni aseru koto nai yo.

④ **You'll get over it.**

そのうち、きっと忘れられるよ。

Sono uchi, kitto wasurerareru yo.

⑤ **It's not your fault.**

あなたが悪いんじゃないからね。

Anata ga warui n' ja nai kara ne.

⑥ **Don't lose your cool.**

冷静に、冷静に。

Reisei ni, reisei ni.

⑦ **You're making a mountain out of a molehill.**

それは、おおげさじゃない？

Sore wa, ōgesa ja nai?

⑧ **Just chill!**

M おちつけ、って！
Ochitsuke tte!

F おちつきなさい、って！
Ochitsukinasai tte!

⑨ **Don't take it personally.**

あなたに対するあてつけじゃないからね。
Anata ni tai suru atetsuke ja nai kara ne.

⑩ **Better luck next time.**

次は、きっと、うまくいくよ。
Tsugi wa kitto umaku iku yo.

# Compliments

MP3

09_11

① **You rock!**

いいねぇ、最高！
Ii nē, saikō!

② **Excellent idea!**

名案！
Meian!

③ **You look great in that blouse.**

そのブラウス、よく似合ってるね。
Sono burausu, yoku niatte 'ru ne.

④ **You're indispensable.**

あなたは、なくてはならない存在です。

Anata wa nakute wa naranai sonzai desu.

⑤ **You crack me up!**

もう、おなかが、よじれそう！

Mō, onaka ga yojiresō!

⑥ **I can't tell you how wonderful you are.**

あなたって、最高ですよ！
ほめ言葉が見つからないくらい！

Anata tte, saikō desu yo!
Homekotoba ga mitsukaranai kurai!

⑦ **Your girlfriend is a knockout.**

M おまえの彼女、すっげえ美人だな。

Omae no kanojo, suggē bijin da na.

⑧ **I hear you're very talented.**

あなたのことは、とても有能な方と
伺っております。

Anata no koto wa, totemo yūnō na kata to
ukagatte orimasu.

⑨ **I know I can depend on you.**

頼りにしてるから、よろしくね。

Tayori ni shite 'ru kara, yoroshiku ne.

# Criticisms

MP3

09_12

---

① **You dork!**

だッさ〜！

Dassā!

---

② **What do you think you're doing?**

いったい、どういうつもり？

Ittai, dō iu tsumori?

---

③ **What's with you? You're acting screwy.**

どうしたの？　やってること、おかしいよ！

Dōshita no? Yatteru koto, okashii yo!

---

④ **You should be ashamed of yourself.**

恥を知りなさい！

Haji o shirinasai!

---

⑤ **What are you, stupid?**

M 何、勘違いしてんだよ、バカ！

Nani kanchigai shite n' da yo, baka!

F 何、勘違いしてんのよ、バカ！

Nani kanchigai shite n' no yo, baka!

---

⑥ **You don't know squat.**

何にもわかってないくせに。

Nanni mo wakatte 'nai kuseni.

⑦ **You need to get with the program.**

時代の空気、読んだら？

Jidai no kūki, yondara?

---

# Insults and Incendiaries

09_13

① **Asshole!**

M バカ野郎！

Bakayarō!

---

② **Fuck off!**

M 失せろ！

Usero!

---

③ **Screw you!**

死ね！

Shine!

---

④ **Let's take it outside.**

M 外に出ろ。

Soto ni dero.

---

⑤ **You want a piece of me?**

M てめえ、やる気か？

Temē, yaruki ka?

---

⑥ **Kiss my ass.**

バ〜カ！

Bāka!

⑦ **Get out of my face.**

M うるせぇ、この野郎。
Urusē, kono yarō.

⑧ **Just shut up.**

M だまれ！
Damare!

F うるさい！
Urusai!

⑨ **Come over here and say that.**

M いまの、もういちど言ってみろ。
Ima no, mō ichido itte miro.

F いまの、もういちど言ってみなさい。
Ima no, mō ichido itte minasai.

# Apologies and Excuses

MP3
09_14

① **I'm so sorry.**
本当に申し訳ありませんでした。
Hontō ni mōshiwake arimasen deshita.

② **I really didn't know.**
本当に知らなかったんです。
Hontō ni shiranakatta n' desu.

③ **That is not what I intended.**

そんなつもりでは、なかったんです。

Sonna tsumori de wa, nakatta n' desu.

④ **Can you accept my apology?**

許していただけますか？

Yurushite itadakemasu ka?

⑤ **How can I make it right?**

どうすれば償えるでしょうか？

Dō sureba tsugunaeru deshō ka?

⑥ **We want to make up for it.**

埋め合わせを、させてもらえませんか？

Umeawase o, sasete moraemasen ka?

⑦ **It won't happen again.**

二度と、このようなことが、ないようにいたします。

Nido to, kono yō na koto ga nai yō ni itashimasu.

# Forgiving and Forgetting

MP3
09_15

① **It's okay.**

いいですよ。

Ii desu yo.

② **We're fine now.**

もう、だいじょうぶです。

Mō, daijōbu desu.

③ **It's really no big deal.**

いいよ、たいしたことじゃないから。

Ii yo, taishita koto ja nai kara.

④ **Now you know.**

わかってくれたなら、いいよ。

Wakattekureta nara, ii yo.

⑤ **It was an honest mistake.**

いいよ、悪気じゃなかったんだから。

Ii yo, warugi ja nakatta n' da kara.

⑥ **It's water under the bridge.**

もう、過ぎたことですから……。

Mō, sugita koto desu kara . . .

⑦ **It'll take some time, but I'll get over it.**

少し時間はかかるけど、
そのうち忘れられると思います。

Sukoshi jikan wa kakaru kedo,
sono uchi wasurerareru to omoimasu.

⑧ **No need to apologize at all.**

謝らなくって、いいんだよ。

Ayamaranakutte, ii n' da yo.

⑨ **Let's just forget about it, okay?**

水に流そうよ、ね？

Mizu ni nagasō yo, ne?

## Happiness

MP3
10_01

① **This feels wonderful!**

あー、いい気もち！

Ā, ii kimochi!

② **This is perfect.**

完ぺきだね！

Kampeki da ne!

③ **What a blast!**

チョー楽しかった！

Chō-tanoshikatta!

④ **That was awesome.**

最高でした！

Saikō deshita!

⑤ **That was hilarious!**

めっちゃ面白かった！

Metcha omoshirokatta!

⑥ **I'm totally impressed.**

すばらしい！ 感動しました。

Subarashii! Kandō shimashita.

⑦ **I'm in a great mood.**
最高の気分です。
Saikō no kibun desu.

⑧ **I'm feeling on top of the world!**
天にも昇る心地です。
Ten ni mo noboru kokochi desu.

## Sadness

10_02

① **I feel lonely.**
淋しいんです……。
Sabishii n' desu . . .

② **It tears me apart.**
胸が張り裂けそうです。
Mune ga harisakesō desu.

③ **I can't stop crying.**
涙が止まらないよ……。
Namida ga tomaranai yo . . .

④ **Things will never be the same.**
もう、これまでとは、ちがうんですね。
Mō, kore made to wa, chigau n' desu ne.

⑤ **I'm heartbroken.**
心がズタズタです……。
Kokoro ga zutazuta desu . . .

MP3
10_03

# Confidence and Determination

① **I'm confident I can do it.**

やれます、自信あります。

Yaremasu, jishin arimasu.

② **This is a sure thing.**

絶対うまくいくよ。

Zettai umaku iku yo.

③ **This is a win-win situation.**

これなら、八方丸くおさまるよ。

Kore nara, happō maruku osamaru yo.

④ **I've got it covered.**

ちゃんと手は打っといたから。

Chanto te wa uttoita kara.

⑤ **Leave it to me.**

任せてください。

Makasete kudasai.

⑧ **I'm up for anything.**

何でも来い、ってところです。

Nandemo koi tte tokoro desu.

⑦ **Trust me.**

だいじょうぶ、信じてください。

Daijōbu, shinjite kudasai.

⑧ **This is something I believe in.**

わたしは、これが正しいことだと思ってますから。

Watashi wa, kore ga tadashii koto da to omotte 'masu kara.

---

⑨ **I've never failed you before.**

これまで、期待を裏切ったことは、なかったでしょう？

Kore made, kitai o uragitta koto wa, nakatta deshō?

---

⑩ **How hard can it be?**

そんなの、たかが知れてるよ。

Sonna no, takaga shirete 'ru yo.

## Gratitude

① **You're so thoughtful.**

気にかけてくれて、本当にありがとう。

Ki ni kakete kurete, hontō ni arigatō.

---

② **That's very generous of you.**

ありがとう。では、お言葉に甘えて……。

Arigatō. De wa, o-kotoba ni amaete . . .

---

③ **How did you manage this?**

感激です、こんなにしてもらって！

Kangeki desu, konna ni shite moratte!

---

④ **You're a lifesaver.**

ありがとう、本当に助かりました。

Arigatō, hontō ni tasukarimashita.

Feelings

⑤ **You just made my day.**

おかげで、すばらしい一日になりました。

Okagede, subarashii ichinichi ni narimashita.

⑥ **How can I ever thank you enough?**

どんなに感謝しても感謝しきれません。

Donna ni kansha shite mo kansha shikiremasen.

⑦ **You're the best!**

本当に、本当に、ありがとう！

Hontō ni, hontō ni, arigatō!

⑧ **I'm in debt to you.**

恩に着ます。

On ni kimasu.

⑨ **I'll never forget your kindness.**

ご親切は、決して忘れません。

Go-shinsetsu wa, kesshite wasuremasen.

# Anxiety

MP3

10_05

① **I've got a bad feeling about this.**

いやな予感がする……。

Iya na yokan ga suru . . .

② **I wonder what's going to happen.**

どうなるのかなぁ……。

Dō naru no ka nā . . .

③ **I'm afraid it won't work.**

うまくいかないんじゃないかなぁ……。

Umaku ikanai n' ja nai ka nā . . .

④ **We are really screwed.**

マジ、やばいよ。

Maji, yabai yo.

⑤ **This doesn't look good.**

まずいね。

Mazui ne.

⑥ **I'm losing sleep over this.**

心配で、眠れないんです。

Shimpai de, nemurenai n' desu.

⑦ **I'm constantly on edge.**

このところ、いつも神経がピリピリしてるんです。

Kono tokoro, itsumo shinkei ga piripiri shite 'ru n' desu.

⑧ **Are you mad at me?**

怒ってるの？

Okotte 'ru no?

# Sympathy

MP3
10_06

① **That sounds like a drag.**

うんざりって感じの話だね。

Unzari tte kanji no hanashi da ne.

② **That really sucks.**

ほんと、最低だよね！

Honto, saitei da yo ne!

③ **I understand how you feel.**

お気もち、わかります。

O-kimochi, wakarimasu.

④ **I hope you get better soon.**

早くよくなりますように。

Hayaku yoku narimasu yō ni.

⑤ **Nothing lasts forever.**

朝の来ない夜はないから……。

Asa no konai yoru wa nai kara . . .

⑥ **I wish I could ease your suffering.**

その苦しみを軽くしてあげられたら、と思います。

Sono kurushimi o karuku shite ageraretara, to omoimasu.

⑦ **My heart aches for you.**

あなたのことを思うと、心が痛みます。

Anata no koto o omou to, kokoro ga itamimasu.

⑧ **Here's a number you can call for help.**

誰かに助けてほしいときは、
ここに電話するといいですよ。

Dareka ni tasukete hoshii toki wa,
koko ni denwa suru to ii desu yo.

# Self-pity and Regret

**Feelings**

① **Nothing ever works out for me.**

やることなすこと、うまくいかないんだから！

Yaru koto nasu koto, umaku ikanai n' dakara!

② **I can't seem to do anything right.**

何をやっても、失敗ばかり！

Nani o yatte mo, shippai bakari!

③ **I really screwed up.**

やっちゃったよ、大失敗！

Yatchatta yo, daishippai!

④ **I never should have done that.**

あんなこと、しなけりゃよかった。

Anna koto, shinakerya yokatta.

⑤ **I tried my best, but I blew it.**

ベストを尽くしたけど、うまくいきませんでした。

Besuto o tsukushita kedo, umaku ikimasen deshita.

⑥ **I should have done something right away.**

すぐに何か手を打つべきでした。

Sugu ni nanika te o utsu beki deshita.

⑦ **I wish this never happened!**

これが夢ならよかったのに！

Kore ga yume nara yokatta no ni!

⑧ **The damage is done.**

もう手遅れです。

Mō teokure desu.

---

# Irritation

10_08

① **I can't stand it anymore!**

もう、がまんできない！

Mō, gaman dekinai!

---

② **What's with that?**

ありえないよ～！

Arienai yō!

---

③ **This place drives me crazy.**

こんなところにいたら、頭、おかしくなりそう！

Konna tokoro ni itara, atama okashiku narisō!

---

④ **Give me a break!**

冗談きついよ！

Jōdan kitsui yo!

---

⑤ **Cut it out!**

M　おい、やめろよ！

Oi, yamero yo!

F　ちょっと、やめてよ！

Chotto, yamete yo!

⑥ **Just forget it.**

もういいから。

Mō ii kara.

⑦ **I've had it up to here with you!**

もう、うんざりだよ！

Mō, unzari da yo!

⑧ **Spare me please.**

かんべんしてくださいよ。

Kamben shite kudasai yo.

⑨ **Don't get high and mighty with me!**

えらそうな口、聞くんじゃない！

Erasō na kuchi, kiku n' ja nai!

⑩ **You're acting like a jerk!**

F いやな人ね！

Iya na hito ne!

⑪ **Would you please stop that?**

それ、やめてもらえませんか？

Sore, yamete moraemasen ka?

⑫ **Don't be such a prick.**

F やーだ、最低！

Yā da, saitei!

⑬ **This is none of your business.**

大きなお世話です。

Ōki na o-sewa desu.

Feelings

⑭ **Just who do you think you are?**

F あんた、何様だと思ってんの？
Anta, nanisama da to omotte n' no?

M おまえ、何様だと思ってるわけ？
Omae, nanisama da to omotteru wake?

# Hope and Excitement

MP3
10_09

① **Keep your fingers crossed!**
うまくいくように、祈ってて！
Umaku iku yō ni, inotte 'te!

② **That's what I'm praying for.**
そうなればいいな、と思ってるんだ。
Sō nareba ii na, to omotte 'ru n' da.

③ **This is my dream come true.**
まさに夢がかなった、という感じです。
Masa ni yume ga kanatta, to iu kanji desu.

④ **I have a good feeling about this.**
うまくいきそうな予感がするよ。
Umaku ikisō na yokan ga suru yo.

⑤ **I can't wait!**
待ち遠しいな！
Machidōshii na!

⑥ **I'm so fired up about this.**

興奮でわくわくしています。

Kōfun de wakuwaku shite imasu.

⑦ **Excellent news!**

すばらしいニュースだね！

Subarashii nyūsu da ne!

⑧ **This is what I've been waiting for.**

これを待ってたんです！

Kore o matte 'ta n' desu!

# Wonder and Curiosity

MP3
10_10

① **That's amazing!**

すっごい！

Suggoi!

② **How did that happen?**

なんでまた、そんなことに……？

Nande mata, sonna koto ni . . . ?

③ **How did you do that?**

どうやったの？

Dō yatta no?

④ **That's so bizarre!**

変な話！

Hen na hanashi!

⑤ **I wonder how that works.**

これ、どうなってるんだろう？

Kore, dō natte 'ru n' darō?

---

⑥ **I'm dying to know what he says.**

彼<ruby>が<rt>かれ</rt></ruby>何て言うか、聞きたくてたまんない。

Kare ga nante iu ka, kikitakute tamannai.

---

⑦ **It's not my business, but I have to know.**

よけいなお世話かもしれないけど、気になるから。

Yokei na o-sewa ka mo shirenai kedo, ki ni naru kara.

---

# Indignation

MP3
10_11

① **WTF!**

ゲッ、何それ！

Ge, nani sore!

---

② **She said what?**

なんだって？

Nan da tte?

---

③ **Take it back!**

M いまの言葉、撤回しろ！

Ima no kotoba, tekkai shiro!

F いまの言葉、撤回しなさいよ！

Ima no kotoba, tekkai shinasai yo!

④ **How can you say that?**

よくも、そんなこと言えるね！

Yokumo, sonna koto ieru ne!

⑤ **The nerve of him!**

よくもまあ、いけしゃあしゃあと！

Yokumo mā, ikeshāshā to!

⑥ **How rude of you!**

この礼儀知らず！

Kono reigi-shirazu!

⑦ **You are way out of line.**

身のほどをわきまえたほうが、いいですよ。

Mi no hodo o wakimaeta hō ga, ii desu yo.

⑧ **How can you be so insensitive?**

どうして、そう無神経なわけ？

Dōshite, sō mushinkei na wake?

⑨ **I'm really pissed off!**

チョー腹立つ！

Chō haratatsu!

# Confusion and Doubt

MP3
10_12

① **I don't get it.**

いまの話、わかんないなぁ。

Ima no hanashi, wakannai nā.

② **Huh?**

ん？

N?

③ **I'm having a senior moment.**

ちょっと待って、ど忘れしちゃった。

Chotto matte, dowasure shichatta.

④ **That's hard to believe.**

ちょっと信じられない話だね。

Chotto shinjirarenai hanashi da ne.

⑤ **That doesn't make any sense.**

理解できないよ！

Rikai dekinai yo!

⑥ **What are we supposed to do now?**

さあ、これからどうする？

Sā, kore kara dō suru?

⑦ **I'm totally confused!**

頭、こんがらがっちゃった！

Atama, kongaragatchatta!

## Indifference

MP3
10_13

① **WhatEVER.**

どうでもいいよ。

Dōdemo ii yo.

② **I couldn't care less.**

どうだって、かまわないね。

Dōdatte, kamawanai ne.

③ **So what?**

だから、何？

Dakara, nani?

④ **Suit yourself.**

勝手にすれば。

Katte ni sureba.

⑤ **It's no skin off my back.**

こっちは痛くもかゆくもないし。

Kotchi wa itaku mo kayuku mo nai shi.

⑥ **Either way is fine with me.**

わたしは、どっちでもかまいませんよ。

Watashi wa, dotchi demo kamaimasen yo.

⑦ **It's no big deal.**

たいした問題じゃないでしょ。

Taishita mondai ja nai desho.

⑧ **It's not worth talking about.**

いちいち話題にするまでもないことです。

Ichiichi wadai ni suru made mo nai koto desu.

⑨ **It's nothing I'm going to lose any sleep over.**

そんなこと、全然、心配じゃないよ。

Sonna koto, zenzen shimpai ja nai yo.

# Shock and Awe

MP3
10_14

① **Oh my God!**

うわっ！

Uwa!

② **Oh, shit!**

ゲッ！

Ge!

③ **I don't believe this.**

うそでしょ……。

Uso desho . . .

④ **What on earth were you thinking?**

ちょっと、何考えてたの？

Chotto, nani kangaete 'ta no?

⑤ **Holy Moly!**

へ〜！

Hē!

⑥ **I'm speechless.**

言葉を失うね……。

Kotoba o ushinau ne . . .

⑦ **How could this have happened?**

どうして、こんなことに、なったんだろう？

Dōshite konna koto ni natta n' darō?

**⑧ What a total nightmare!**

こりゃ、まさに悪夢だ！

Korya, masa ni akumu da!

## Weariness and Wellness

MP3
10_15

**① I'm dead tired.**

もう、へっとへと……。

Mō, hettoheto . . .

**② I'm hungover.**

きょうは二日酔いなんだ。

Kyō wa futsukayoi nan da.

**③ I'm completely burnt out.**

疲れた〜、もうだめだ〜。

Tsukaretā, mō dame dā.

**④ This is killing me.**

これはキツイ！

Kore wa kitsui!

**⑤ I can't go another step.**

もう一歩も歩けないよ。

Mō ippo mo arukenai yo.

**⑥ I'm in top form.**

体調は万全です。

Taichō wa banzen desu.

⑦ **I've got energy to burn.**
元気、あり余ってるから！
Genki, ariamatte 'ru kara!

⑧ **I've never felt better.**
絶好調です。
Zekkōchō desu.

⑨ **I'm good to go!**
準備万端です！
Jumbi-bantan desu!

# Depression and Trauma

① **I'm so depressed I can't get out of bed.**
気分が落ち込んで、ベッドから
出られなくて……。
Kibun ga ochikonde, beddo kara
derarenakute . . .

② **I need someone to talk to.**
だれか、話し相手がほしい……。
Dareka, hanashi-aite ga hoshii . . .

③ **I'm working myself to the bone.**
毎日、身を粉にして働いてるんです。
Mainichi, mi o ko ni shite hataraite 'ru n' desu.

④ **My husband is being abusive.**

夫から暴力を受けているんです。

Otto kara bōryoku o ukete iru n' desu.

⑤ **My wife is having an affair.**

M 妻が浮気してるんです。

Tsuma ga uwaki shite 'ru n' desu.

⑥ **My daughter is being bullied at school.**

娘が学校でいじめにあってるんです。

Musume ga gakkō de ijime ni atte 'ru n' desu.

⑦ **I've lost my will to live.**

もう、生きる気力がなくなりました。

Mō, ikiru kiryoku ga nakunarimashita.

⑧ **Do you know where I can get help?**

どこか助けてもらえるところ、知りませんか？

Dokoka tasukete moraeru tokoro, shirimasen ka?

⑨ **I need someone to go with me.**

だれか、一緒に行ってほしいんだけど……。

Dareka, issho ni itte hoshii n' da kedo . . .

---

### Stating Your State

In English, to say you are sleepy, smart, or angry is incredibly easy. Just say, "I'm" and add the vocabulary word. In Japanese, there are frequently a variety of constructions you can use to describe your situation. In some cases, the sensation is linked by language to the physical root of the sensation, and this makes the expression a bit easier to visualize and remember:

| | |
|---|---|
| **onaka ga suite iru** | my stomach is empty (= I'm hungry) |
| **nodo ga kawaite iru** | my throat has dried (= I'm thirsty) |
| **hara ga tatte iru** | my stomach is standing up (= I'm offended) |
| **me ga mawatte iru** | my eyes are spinning (= I'm dizzy) |

In other cases, the Japanese is nearly as easy as the English, with **iru** standing in for an informal "I'm" plus a verb.

| | |
|---|---|
| **yorokonde iru** | I'm delighted |
| **osoku natte iru** | I'm late |
| **okotte iru** | I'm angry |
| **tsukarete iru** | I'm tired |
| **manzoku shite iru** | I'm satisfied |

Some states are simple adjectives in Japanese, optionally followed by **desu**.

| | |
|---|---|
| **ureshii (desu)** | I'm happy |
| **nemui (desu)** | I'm sleepy |

And finally, there are idiomatic expressions that deal with the state of the spirit, or one's feeling, which is in Japanese **ki** or **kibun**:

| | |
|---|---|
| **ki ga nai** | I'm uninterested |
| **ki ga omoi** | I'm bummed out |
| **ki ga susumanai** | I'm reluctant |
| **ki ga tōku naru** | I'm overwhelmed |
| **kibun ga warui** | I feel bad |
| **kibun ga ii** | I feel good |

At first you might feel **ki ga tōku naru**, but it won't take long before you are using these phrases with ease!

# On the Job

① **What's it like working here?**
この職場は、どんな感じですか？
Kono shokuba wa, donna kanji desu ka?

② **What kind of jobs are available?**
どんな仕事がありますか？
Donna shigoto ga arimasu ka?

③ **What's the pay like?**
お給料は、どのくらいですか？
O-kyūryō wa, dono kurai desu ka?

④ **What are the hours?**
就業時間は、何時から何時までですか？
Shūgyōjikan wa, nanji kara nanji made desu ka?

⑤ **What qualifications do I need?**
どんな資格が必要ですか？
Donna shikaku ga hitsuyō desu ka?

⑥ **Where is the main office located?**
本社はどこですか？
Honsha wa doko desu ka?

⑦ **Are there any benefits included?**

手当も含まれていますか？

Teate mo fukumarete imasu ka?

⑧ **Is the position part-time or full-time?**

その仕事はパートですか？ フルタイムですか？

Sono shigoto wa pāto desu ka? Furu taimu desu ka?

⑨ **How long is the contract for?**

契約期間は、どのくらいですか？

Keiyaku kikan wa, dono kurai desu ka?

⑩ **When would I start?**

何日から出勤することになりますか？

Nannichi kara shukkin suru koto ni narimasu ka?

# Setting Up an Interview

MP3
11_02

① **I'm calling about your employment ad.**

御社の求人広告を見て、お電話しました。

Onsha no kyūjin-kōkoku o mite, o-denwa shimashita.

② **Is the manager position still open?**

マネージャーの求人は、まだ締め切ってませんか？

Manējā no kyūjin wa, mada shimekitte 'masen ka?

③ **I'd like to apply for the teaching job.**

教師の求人に応募したいのですが。

Kyōshi no kyūjin ni ōbo shitai no desu ga.

④ **I'd be happy to come in anytime this week.**

今週でしたら、どの日でも伺えます。

Konshū deshitara, dono hi demo ukagaemasu.

⑤ **What documents should I bring?**

どういった書類を用意すれば、よろしいですか？

Dō itta shorui o yōi sureba yoroshii desu ka?

⑥ **Does my resume need to be in Japanese?**

履歴書は、日本語で書いたほうが、よろしいですか？

Rirekisho wa, Nihongo de kaita hō ga yoroshii desu ka?

⑦ **I have a valid work visa.**

就労ビザを持っております。

Shūrō biza o motte orimasu.

⑧ **May I send you my CV ahead of time?**

あらかじめ履歴書をお送りしても、

よろしいでしょうか？

Arakajime rirekisho o ookuri shite mo,
yoroshii deshō ka?

⑨ **Monday morning at eight sounds perfect.**

月曜、朝8時ですね？　承知しました。

Getsuyō, asa hachiji desu ne? Shōchi shimashita.

⑩ **Do I need to take any qualifying tests?**

採用試験などは、ありますか？

Saiyō-shiken nado wa, arimasu ka?

# The Interview

MP3
11_03

① **Thank you very much for seeing me.**

きょうはお時間をいただき、ありがとうございます。

Kyō wa o-jikan o itadaki, arigatō gozaimasu.

② **I'm a motivated and quick learner.**

わたしはモチベーションも高いですし、
仕事の飲み込みも早いです。

Watashi wa mochibēshon mo takai desu shi,
shigoto no nomikomi mo hayai desu.

③ **I've worked in this field for many years.**

この分野なら、長年の経験があります。

Kono bun'ya nara, naganen no keiken ga arimasu.

④ **I've brought my portfolio, if you'd like to see it.**

これまでの実績をまとめた資料を持参しました。
こちらです。

Kore made no jisseki o matometa shiryō o jisan
shimashita. Kochira desu.

⑤ **My skills include copyediting and proofreading.**

原稿の整理や校正もできます。

Genkō no seiri ya kōsei mo dekimasu.

⑥ **I'm looking for a real challenge.**

やりがいのある仕事を求めています。

Yarigai no aru shigoto o motomete imasu.

⑦ **I believe in developing a strong team spirit.**

強力なチーム・スピリットを育てることが重要
と考えています。

Kyōryoku na chīmu-supiritto o sodateru koto ga jūyō to
kangaete imasu.

⑧ **I can start right away.**

いますぐ、始められます。

Ima sugu, hajimeraremasu.

## Comments, Questions, and Self-assessments

**MP3**

11_04

① **I'm looking for full-time employment.**

フルタイムの仕事を探しています。

Furutaimu no shigoto o sagashite imasu.

② **I have young kids, so I'd need daytime shifts.**

子供たちがまだ小さいので、
昼間のシフトでお願いしたいです。

Kodomotachi ga mada chīsai no de,
hiruma no shifuto de onegai shitai desu.

③ **I'd be very willing to take on business travel.**

出張も、まったく問題ありません。

Shutchō mo, mattaku mondai arimasen.

④ **I plan to finish my degree by next year.**

来年までに学位を取得できる見込みです。

Rainen made ni gakui o shutoku dekiru mikomi desu.

⑤ **I plan to be in Japan for several years.**

数年は日本にいるつもりです。

Sūnen wa Nihon ni iru tsumori desu.

⑥ **Do you offer on-the-job training?**

こちらの会社では、オン・ザ・ジョブ・

トレーニングはありますか？

Kochira no kaisha de wa, onzajobu-
torēningu wa arimasu ka?

⑦ **What daily requirements will I need to meet?**

一日のノルマはどのくらいですか？

Ichinichi no noruma wa dono kurai desu ka?

⑧ **I'm ready and willing to improve my Japanese.**

日本語が上達するよう
努力を惜しまない所存です。

Nihongo ga jōtatsu suru yō
doryoku o oshimanai shozon desu.

⑨ **My strength is in market analysis.**

わたしの得意分野は、市場分析です。

Watashi no tokui-bun'ya wa, shijō-bunseki desu.

⑩ **I'm punctual, efficient, and enthusiastic.**

わたしは時間に正確ですし、
仕事も手早いですし、熱意もあります。

Watashi wa jikan ni seikaku desu shi,

shigoto mo tebayai desu shi, netsui mo arimasu.

## On the Job

MP3

11_05

① **Are things always this crazy?**

いつも、こんなめちゃくちゃに忙しいんですか？

Itsumo, konna mechakucha ni isogashii n' desu ka?

② **I think I should handle that.**

わたしが処理しましょう。

Watashi ga shori shimashō.

③ **I can't take on any more work right now.**

いま、ちょっと、手いっぱいです。

Ima, chotto, te-ippai desu.

④ **I have a meeting today.**

きょうは会議があります。

Kyō wa kaigi ga arimasu.

On the Job

⑤ **Can you check over this for me?**

これ、チェック、お願いできますか？

Kore, chekku, onegai dekimasu ka?

⑥ **These numbers don't look right.**

この数字、何かおかしくありませんか？

Kono sūji, nanika okashiku arimasen ka?

⑦ **You'll have to show me how to do that.**

やり方、教えてくださいね。

Yarikata, oshiete kudasai ne.

⑧ **Maybe we should try a different approach.**

ちがうアプローチを試してみましょうか？

Chigau apurōchi o tameshite mimashō ka?

⑨ **We're doing very well this month.**

今月は、かなり好調だね。

Kongetsu wa, kanari kōchō da ne.

## To and From the Office

MP3
11_06

① **Do you always come to work this early?**

いつも、こんな早い時間に出社するんですか？

Itsumo, konna hayai jikan ni shussha suru n' desu ka?

② **What's on the schedule for today?**

きょうのスケジュールは？

Kyō no sukejūru wa?

③ **I have a doctor's appointment, so I'll be late.**

きょうは医者に寄るので、出社が遅くなります。

Kyō wa isha ni yoru no de, shussha ga osoku narimasu.

④ **How long will you be out of the office?**

お休みは、いつまでですか？

O-yasumi wa, itsumade desu ka?

⑤ **I'm going to meet a client over lunch.**

きょうは、お得意さんと昼食の予定です。

Kyō wa, otokuisan to chūshoku no yotei desu.

⑥ **I think I forgot to clock in.**

タイムレコーダー、押し忘れたかも……。

Taimu-rekōdā, oshiwasureta ka mo . . .

⑦ **I have to run this over to accounting.**

これ、急ぎで経理へ届けないと。

Kore, isogi de keiri e todokenai to.

⑧ **We'll be working on this all night.**

この仕事、徹夜になりそうだね。

Kono shigoto, tetsuya ni narisō da ne.

On the Job

# Telephone Calls

11_07

① **I'd like to speak to Mr. Suzuki, if he's in today.**

鈴木さんがおいででしたら、お願いしたいのですが。

Suzuki-san ga oide deshitara, onegai shitai no desu ga.

② **This is Joe Adler calling for Mr. Sato.**

わたくし、ジョー・アドラーと申します。
佐藤さんをお願いしたいのですが。

Watakushi, Jō Adorā to mōshimasu.
Satō-san o onegai shitai no desu ga.

③ **Can you transfer me to your PR division?**

広報部に回していただけますか？

Kōhōbu ni mawashite itadakemasu ka?

④ **May I leave him a message?**

メッセージをお伝えいただけますか？

Messēji o otsutae itadakemasu ka?

⑤ **Have him call me back at this number please.**

この番号に折り返しお電話くださるよう、
お伝えください。

Kono bangō ni orikaeshi o-denwa kudasaru yō,
otsutae kudasai.

⑥ **Just one moment please, I'll see if she's here.**

少々お待ちください、近くにいるかどうか
見てまいります。

Shōshō omachi kudasai, chikaku ni iru ka dō ka
mite mairimasu.

⑦ **He's out. Shall I have him call you back?**

ただいま席をはずしております。折り返し
お電話させましょうか?

Tadaima seki o hazushite orimasu. Orikaeshi
o-denwa sasemashō ka?

⑧ **Let me transfer your call to her section.**

所属の部署へ、お回しいたします。

Shozoku no busho e, omawashi itashimasu.

⑨ **I'll have him get back to you as soon as possible.**

取り急ぎ、本人から連絡させるようにいたします。

Toriisogi, honnin kara renraku saseru yō ni itashimasu.

## Meetings, Memos, Functions, and E-mail

① **Did you see the memo about the meeting?**

会議のメモ、ご覧になりましたか?

Kaigi no memo, goran ni narimashita ka?

② **That room is reserved for a board meeting today.**

その部屋は、きょうの取締役会用に
押さえてあります。

Sono heya wa, kyō no torishimariyakukai-yō ni
osaete arimasu.

③ **We're holding the planning meeting tomorrow.**

明日、企画会議があります。

Asu, kikaku kaigi ga arimasu.

④ **Can I add something to the agenda?**

議題に二、三、付け加えてもよろしいですか？

Gidai ni ni, san, tsukekuwaete mo yoroshii desu ka?

⑤ **Next week we have a party for new employees.**

来週、新入社員の歓迎会があります。

Raishū, shinnyū-shain no kangeikai ga arimasu.

⑥ **Do I have to attend the ceremony?**

式には、わたしも出なくてはいけませんか？

Shiki ni wa, watashi mo denakute wa ikemasen ka?

⑦ **Did you get the e-mail about the year-end party?**

忘年会のメール、届きましたか？

Bōnenkai no mēru, todokimashita ka?

# Contracts, Salaries, Wages, and Benefits

MP3
11_09

① **Does the contract include medical insurance?**

この契約には、健康保険が含まれていますか？

Kono keiyaku ni wa, kenkō-hoken ga fukumarete imasu ka?

② **How many days of paid holidays can I get?**

有給休暇は何日もらえるんでしょうか？

Yūkyū-kyūka wa nannichi moraeru n' deshō ka?

③ **Am I going to be paid for overtime?**

残業代は出ますか？

Zangyōdai wa demasu ka?

---

④ **Is this contract renewable?**

契約の更新は、ありますか？

Keiyaku no kōshin wa, arimasu ka?

---

⑤ **Am I allowed a full maternity leave?**

産休は、規定どおりに取れますか？

Sankyū wa, kitei dōri ni toremasu ka?

---

⑥ **Are there any fringe benefits?**

フリンジ・ベネフィットは、何かありますか？

Furinji-benefitto wa, nanika arimasu ka?

---

⑦ **Will I receive any educational training?**

研修は、ありますか？

Kenshū wa, arimasu ka?

---

⑧ **Will my wages increase eventually?**

いずれ、昇給はあるんでしょうか？

Izure, shōkyū wa aru n' deshō ka?

---

⑨ **Do I get a bonus?**

ボーナスは出ますか？

Bōnasu wa demasu ka?

---

⑩ **I'd like to be considered for a promotion.**

わたくしの昇進を検討していただけませんか？

Watakushi no shōkyū o kentō shite itadakemasen ka?

# Working Well or Working Hell

11_10

① **Can you show me how to do this correctly?**

お手本を見せてもらえますか？

O-tehon o misete moraemasu ka?

② **Are there any dangers involved?**

危険なことは、ありますか？

Kiken na koto wa, arimasu ka?

③ **Does this meet all your expectations?**

不十分な点はありませんか？

Fujūbun na ten wa arimasen ka?

④ **How can I improve my performance?**

もっと実力をつけるには、
何をしたらいいでしょうか？

Motto jitsuryoku o tsukeru ni wa,
nani o shitara ii deshō ka?

⑤ **I'd like to take on more responsibilities.**

わたしの裁量範囲を、もう少し広げて
いただきたいんです。

Watashi no sairyō-han'i o mō sukoshi hirogete
itadakitai n' desu.

⑥ **I'm not getting paid enough to do this.**

この仕事に見合う給料は、もらっていません。

Kono shigoto ni miau kyūryō wa, moratte imasen.

⑦ **I really hate this job.**

こんな仕事、いやでいやでたまんないよ。

Konna shigoto, iya de iya de tamannai yo.

⑧ **I'm going to start looking for another position.**

別の仕事を探そうかと思ってるんだ。

Betsu no shigoto o sagasō ka to omotte 'ru n' da.

⑨ **I think this company has unfair labor practices.**

この会社の働かせ方は、不当だと思います。

Kono kaisha no hatarakasekata wa, futō da to omoimasu.

⑩ **I quit!**

わたくし、やめさせていただきます！

Watakushi, yamesasete itadakimasu!

**On the Job**

## Apartment Hunting

**12_01**

① **I need a two-bedroom place under 200,000 yen.**

家賃20万以下の2LDKを探しています。

Yachin nijūman ika no nī-eru-dī-kē o sagashite imasu.

② **Is the building earthquake safe?**

この建物は、地震が来てもだいじょうぶですか？

Kono tatemono wa, jishin ga kite mo daijōbu desu ka?

③ **We want a place in a quiet neighborhood.**

静かな住宅街の物件が希望です。

Shizuka na jūtakugai no bukken ga kibō desu.

④ **We'd like to look at some floor plans.**

間取りを見たいのですが。

Madori o mitai no desu ga.

⑤ **I need a modern studio apartment near Ginza.**

銀座の近くで、モダンな感じのワンルーム・
マンションを探しています。

Ginza no chikaku de, modan na kanji no wanrūmu-
manshon o sagashite imasu.

⑥ **We're looking to rent a house.**

戸建の賃貸を探しています。

Kodate no chintai o sagashite imasu.

⑦ **My friend and I would like to share a flat.**

友だちと二人でアパートを借りたいんですけど。

Tomodachi to futari de apāto o karitai n' desu kedo.

⑧ **Our main priority is space.**

いちばん重要なのは、広さです。

Ichiban jūyō na no wa, hirosa desu.

⑨ **That looks great, but it's not in my budget.**

いい物件なんだけど、予算オーバーです。

Ii bukken nan da kedo, yosan-ōbā desu.

⑩ **Ideally we want a balcony or a nice view.**

理想を言うなら、バルコニー付きか、
眺めのいい物件がいいです。

Risō o iu nara, barukonī-tsuki ka,

nagame no ii bukken ga ii desu.

## The Walk-through

MP3

12_02

① **This is spacious, but it's also pretty dark.**

広いけど、日当たりが悪いですね。

Hiroi kedo, hiatari ga warui desu ne.

② **The location is perfect, but it feels cramped.**
立地は完ぺきだけど、ちょっと狭いかな。
Ritchi wa kampeki da kedo, chotto semai ka na.

③ **Would we be allowed to refurbish the interior?**
室内をリフォームしてもいいですか？
Shitsunai o rifōmu shite mo ii desu ka?

④ **It seems like this place needs some repairs.**
あちこち修理が必要なようですね。
Achikochi shūri ga hitsuyō na yō desu ne.

⑤ **Is there another electricity outlet?**
このほかにも、コンセント、ありますか？
Kono hoka ni mo, konsento, arimasu ka?

⑥ **Is the owner planning to rent it "as is"?**
大家さんは「現状」のまま貸すつもりですか？
Ōya-san wa "genjō" no mama kasu tsumori desu ka?

⑦ **How do you operate this kind of heater?**
このヒーターは、どうやって使うんですか？
Kono hītā wa, dō yatte tsukau n' desu ka?

⑧ **Is there any major construction planned nearby?**
そばに大きな建物が建つ予定はありますか？
Soba ni ōki na tatemono ga tatsu yotei wa arimasu ka?

⑨ **I'd like to check the water pressure.**
水圧をチェックさせてもらえますか？
Suiatsu o chekku sasete moraemasu ka?

⑩ **Are we allowed to have parties here?**

部屋でパーティーを開くのは、かまいませんか？

Heya de pātī o hiraku no wa, kamaimasen ka?

⑪ **Have these air-conditioners been cleaned?**

エアコンは、クリーニング済みですか？

Eakon wa, kurīningu-zumi desu ka?

---

# Follow-up Questions

MP3
12_03

① **Is there any kind of furniture we can't use on the tatami?**

畳の上に置いてはいけない家具は、ありますか？

Tatami no ue ni oite wa ikenai kagu wa, arimasu ka?

② **This bath looks complicated. How does it work?**

このお風呂はややこしそうだけど、
どうやって使うんですか？

Kono o-furo wa yayakoshisō da kedo,
dō yatte tsukau n' desu ka?

③ **What is the best escape route in case of a fire?**

火事のときの避難経路は？

Kaji no toki no hinan-keiro wa?

④ **How can I contact the apartment manager?**

管理人さんの連絡先は？

Kanrinin-san no renrakusaki wa?

**Home Sweet Home**

⑤ **Can I install my own security system?**
自前でセキュリティ・システムを
付けてもいいですか？
Jimae de sekyuritī-shisutemu o
tsukete mo ii desu ka?

⑥ **Are pets allowed here?**
ペットは飼えますか？
Petto wa kaemasu ka?

# Checking and Signing

MP3

12_04

① **Can we meet the landlord in person?**
大家さんに直接お会いすることは、できますか？
Ōya-san ni chokusetsu oai suru koto wa, dekimasu ka?

② **How much is the deposit, key money, and realtor fee?**
敷金、礼金、仲介手数料は、いくらですか？
Shikikin, reikin, chūkai-tesūryō wa, ikura desu ka?

③ **Will I get any part of my deposit back?**
敷金は、いくらか戻ってくるんでしょうか？
Shikikin wa, ikuraka modotte kuru n' deshō ka?

④ **Can my coworker serve as my guarantor?**
保証人は、会社の同僚でもいいですか？
Hoshōnin wa, kaisha no dōryō demo ii desu ka?

⑤ **Who should I call if something breaks?**

何か故障したときの連絡先は？

Nani ka koshō shita toki no renrakusaki wa?

⑥ **I'm not sure what this means, right here.**

ここに書いてあることの意味が、

よくわからないんですが……。

Kokoni kaite aru koto no imi ga,

yoku wakaranai n' desu ga . . .

⑦ **Can we perhaps negotiate the rent?**

家賃、もう少し安くなりませんか？

Yachin, mō sukoshi yasuku narimasen ka?

⑧ **On what day each month is the rent due?**

家賃は、毎月何日までに

支払えばいいですか？

Yachin wa, maitsuki nannichi made ni

shiharaeba ii desu ka?

⑨ **Is there a monthly management fee?**

毎月の管理費は、かかりますか？

Maitsuki no kanrihi wa, kakarimasu ka?

⑩ **Is there a place to park my motorcycle?**

オートバイを止める場所はありますか？

Ōtobai o tomeru basho wa arimasu ka?

Home Sweet Home

⑪ **Can we renew the lease after two years?**

賃貸契約は2年後に更新できますか？

Chintai keiyaku wa ninengo ni kōshin dekimasu ka?

⑫ **Are the promised repairs included in writing?**

そちらで修繕してくれる箇所は、
書面に記載されていますか？

Sochira de shūzen shite kureru kasho wa,
shomen ni kisai sarete imasu ka?

⑬ **What's my total initial layout in fees and rent?**

部屋代と諸費用で、最初に必要なお金は

いくらになりますか？

Heyadai to shohiyō de, saisho ni hitsuyō na o-kane wa
ikura ni narimasu ka?

⑭ **Let me have my lawyer check over the details.**

うちの弁護士に契約の詳細を

チェックさせたいんですけど。

Uchi no bengoshi ni keiyaku no shōsai o
chekku sasetai n' desu kedo.

⑮ **Where do I sign?**

どこにサインしますか？

Doko ni sain shimasu ka?

# Electricity, Gas, and Water

12_05

① **These exposed wires are dangerous.**

こことか、そことか、電線がむき出しで
危ないですね。

Koko to ka, soko to ka, densen ga mukidashi de
abunai desu ne.

② **Where's the circuit breaker?**

ブレーカーは、どこですか？

Burēkā wa, doko desu ka?

③ **Can I change the light fixtures here?**

照明器具を付け替えてもいいですか？

Shōmei-kigu o tsukekaete mo ii desu ka?

④ **What is the voltage rate here?**

ここの電圧は何ボルトですか？

Koko no den'atsu wa nan boruto desu ka?

⑤ **Where's the gas shut-off valve?**

ガスの元栓は、どこですか？

Gasu no motosen wa, doko desu ka?

⑧ **Is the gas system here LPG or city?**

ここのガスは、プロパンですか？　都市ガスですか？

Koko no gasu wa, puropan desu ka? Toshi gasu desu ka?

⑦ **Where's the water boiler?**

ボイラーはどこにありますか？

Boirā wa doko ni arimasu ka?

⑧ **I can't find my water-service application card.**

水道の申込書が見あたらないんですけど。

Suidō no mōshikomisho ga miataranai n' desu kedo.

## Repairs and Complaints

MP3
12_06

① **There's a leak here.**

ここ、漏れてます。

Koko, morete 'masu.

② **The kitchen sink has become badly clogged.**

台所の排水管が詰まって、流れないんです。

Daidokoro no haisuikan ga tsumatte, nagarenai n' desu.

③ **This place is overrun with roaches!**

この部屋、ゴキブリだらけじゃないですか！

Kono heya, gokiburi-darake ja nai desu ka!

④ **I think I may need a rat exterminator.**

ネズミの駆除を頼んだほうがいいかな。

Nezumi no kujo o tanonda hō ga ii ka na.

⑤ **My neighbors are noisy.**

となりがうるさいんです。

Tonari ga urusai n' desu.

⑥ **These repairs were specified in the lease.**

この修理は、契約に書いてありますよね。

Kono shūri wa, keiyaku ni kaite arimasu yo ne.

---

⑦ **My apartment has been burglarized.**

部屋にドロボウがはいったんです。

Heya ni dorobō ga haitta n' desu.

---

⑧ **I was cooking, and the fire alarm went off.**

料理してたら、火災報知器が鳴ったんです。

Ryōri shite 'tara, kasai-hōchiki ga natta n' desu.

---

⑨ **These windows don't open.**

ここの窓、開かないんですけど。

Koko no mado, akanai n' desu kedo.

---

⑩ **There's a lot of mildew and mold here.**

ここ、結露がひどくて、カビが生えています。

Koko, ketsuro ga hidokute, kabi ga haete imasu.

---

# Services and Facilities

MP3
12_07

① **What day is burnable garbage collected?**

「燃えるゴミ」は、何曜日ですか？

"Moeru gomi" wa, nan'yōbi desu ka?

---

② **Is this considered non-burnable garbage?**

これは「燃えないゴミ」になりますか？

Kore wa "moenai gomi" ni narimasu ka?

③ **What do we do with recyclables?**

資源ゴミは、
どうやって出せばいいですか？

Shigen-gomi wa,
dō yatte daseba ii desu ka?

④ **Do we separate newspapers and magazines?**

新聞と雑誌は、分別して出すんですか？

Shimbun to zasshi wa, bumbetsu shite dasu n' desu ka?

⑤ **Is there a special fee to use the storage room?**

倉庫を借りると、別に使用料がかかりますか？

Sōko o kariru to, betsu ni shiyōryō ga kakarimasu ka?

⑥ **Are we allowed to barbecue here?**

ここでバーベキューをしてもいいですか？

Koko de bābekyū o shite mo ii desu ka?

⑦ **When is the next fire inspection?**

こんどの消防検査は、いつですか？

Kondo no shōbō-kensa wa, itsu desu ka?

⑧ **What does the water pipes inspection involve?**

水道の点検って、何をするんですか？

Suidō no tenken tte, nani o suru n' desu ka?

⑨ **Will you tell me when a parking spot opens up?**

駐車場に空きが出たら、声をかけてもらえますか？

Chūshajō ni aki ga detara, koe o kakete moraemasu ka?

⑩ **Is there a charge for parking my bicycle?**

駐輪場は、有料ですか？

Chūrinjō wa, yūryō desu ka?

## Logistic Details

12_08

① **What should I do if I lose my key?**

鍵をなくしたときは、どうすればいいですか？

Kagi o nakushita toki wa, dō sureba ii desu ka?

② **Is there access for the handicapped?**

出入口など、バリアフリーになっていますか？

Deiriguchi nado, bariafurī ni natte imasu ka?

③ **What happens if a package comes and I'm out?**

宅配の荷物が届いたときに留守だったら、

どうなりますか？

Takuhai no nimotsu ga todoita toki ni rusu dattara,
dō narimasu ka?

④ **Can you tell me a little about my neighbors?**

ご近所は、どんな方たちですか？

Go-kinjo wa, donna katatachi desu ka?

Home Sweet Home

⑤ **Where's the nearest daycare center?**

いちばん近いデイケア・センターは、

どこにありますか？

Ichiban chikai deikea-sentā wa,
doko ni arimasu ka?

⑥ **Can you tell me what this notice means?**

この「お知らせ」、何て書いてあるのか、

教えてくれませんか？

Kono "oshirase," nante kaite aru no ka,
oshiete kuremasen ka?

⑦ **Who's responsible for cleaning the hall?**

玄関ホールの掃除は、だれがしてくれるのですか？

Genkan-hōru no sōji wa, dare ga shite kureru no desu ka?

# Moving In

12_09

① **Please be careful with that.**

それ、気を付けて運んでくださいね！

Sore, ki o tsukete hakonde kudasai ne!

② **I'm not sure how to get this sofa in the door!**

このソファ、ドアを通るかな……？

Kono sofa, doa o tōru ka na . . . ?

③ **Hi, I'm Kylie Walker,**
**your new neighbor, in room 203.**

初めまして。こんど203号室に越してきた
カイリー・ウォーカーと申します。

Hajimemashite. Kondo ni-maru-san-gōshitsu ni koshite kita
Kairī Wōkā to mōshimasu.

---

④ **Sorry for the noise as I was moving in.**

引っ越しでお騒がせして、すみません。

Hikkoshi de osawagase shite, sumimasen.

---

⑤ **Here's a small token of my good will.**

これは、ご挨拶のしるしです。

Kore wa, go-aisatsu no shirushi desu.

---

⑥ **Where can I get a nameplate like this?**

こういう表札は、どこで売っていますか？

Kō iu hyōsatsu wa, doko de utte imasu ka?

---

⑦ **Come check out my new digs.**

新しい部屋に引っ越したんだ。見に来て！

Atarashii heya ni hikkoshita n' da. Mi ni kite!

---

⑧ **Please join our housewarming party.**

新居のおひろめをしたいので、
どうぞお越しください。

Shinkyo no ohirome o shitai no de,
dōzo okoshi kudasai.

**Home Sweet Home**

⑨ **I've got to send out change-of-address postcards.**

引っ越しあいさつの葉書、出さなくちゃ。

Hikkoshi aisatsu no hagaki, dasanakucha.

---

### Apartment Details

The average apartment in Japan is less than 100 square meters, comes unfurnished and often with no major appliances (refrigerator, stove, oven, etc.). Traditional digs may include **oshiire** (large closets for bedding), **fusuma** (sliding paper doors), and sometimes **shoji** (partitioned doors with paper-covered panels) or **tatami** (rush straw mats).

Rentals are usually listed with the number of rooms, plus abbreviations indicating additional facilities, if any. A "2LDK" means a two-bedroom place with a combined one-room "dining/living/kitchen" space. Sometimes rooms are measured by the number of tatami mats that will fit inside; a **roku-jo**, or six-mat-sized room, for example is approximately 9 m$^2$.

# Getting Stuff Done

## At Home

MP3

13_01

① **Let's tidy up.**

少しかたづけようか。

Sukoshi katazukeyō ka.

② **Did you fill the bath?**

お風呂、入れてくれた？

O-furo, irete kureta?

③ **We need to buy toilet paper.**

トイレットペーパー、買わなくちゃ。

Toiretto pēpā, kawanakucha.

④ **I'll do the dishes.**

F 洗いもの、わたしがやるわ。

Araimono, watashi ga yaru wa.

M 洗いもの、ぼくがやるよ。

Araimono, boku ga yaru yo.

⑤ **We need to get rid of all this trash.**

このゴミ、ぜんぶ捨ててこなくちゃ。

Kono gomi, zembu sutete konakucha.

⑥ **Close the door.**

ドア、閉めて。

Doa, shimete.

⑦ **Make the bed.**

ベッド、きれいに直して。

Beddo, kirei ni naoshite.

⑧ **Help me find my keys.**

ねぇ、わたしの鍵、知らない?

Nē, watashi no kagi, shiranai?

⑨ **Don't forget to turn off the gas.**

ガス、ちゃんと止めてね。

Gasu, chanto tomete ne.

# At the Bank

MP3
13_02

① **I'd like to open a regular savings account.**

普通預金の口座を開きたいんですけど。

Futsūyokin no kōza o hirakitai n' desu kedo.

② **Do you require a minimum monthly balance?**

毎月、一定の預金残高が必要ですか?

Maitsuki, ittei no yokin-zandaka ga hitsuyō desu ka?

③ **My cash card doesn't seem to be working.**

キャッシュ・カードが使えないんです。

Kyasshu-kādo ga tsukaenai n' desu.

④ **I need to make a large withdrawal today.**

きょう、大きい金額を引き出したいのですが。

Kyō, ōkii kingaku o hikidashitai no desu ga.

⑤ **Can I apply for a credit card here?**

クレジット・カードの申し込みは、

ここでできますか？

Kurejitto-kādo no mōshikomi wa,
koko de dekimasu ka?

⑥ **Where's the foreign exchange?**

両替は、どこですか？

Ryōgae wa, doko desu ka?

⑦ **What is the exchange rate on sterling today?**

きょうの為替レートは、1ポンド何円ですか？

Kyō no kawase-rēto wa, ichipondo nan'en desu ka?

⑧ **I'm interested in a multicurrency account.**

マルチ・カレンシー口座に関心があります。

Maruchi-karenshī kōza ni kyōmi ga arimasu.

⑨ **I'd like to purchase traveler's checks.**

トラベラーズ・チェックを購入したいんですけど。

Toraberāzu-chekku o kōnyū shitai n' desu kedo.

⑩ **I need to check my savings balance.**

預金残高をチェックしたいんですが。

Yokin-zandaka o chekku shitai n' desu ga.

⑪ **My passbook pages are full.**
通帳がいっぱいになりました。
Tsūchō ga ippai ni narimashita.

⑫ **I need to make a bank transfer.**
お金を振り込みたいんですけど。
O-kane o furikomitai n' desu kedo.

⑬ **How much does it cost to transfer money?**
振り込み手数料は、いくらかかりますか？
Furikomi-tesūryō wa, ikura kakarimasu ka?

⑭ **I need a receipt of the transfer.**
振り込みの控えをください。
Furikomi no hikae o kudasai.

⑮ **I'd like to send funds to my office in Paris.**
パリの法人口座に送金できますか？
Pari no hōjin-kōza ni sōkin dekimasu ka?

⑯ **What's the cheapest way to wire money to New York?**
ニューヨークに送金したいんですが、
どういう方法がいちばん安いですか？
Nyūyōku ni sōkin shitai n' desu ga,
dō iu hōhō ga ichiban yasui desu ka?

⑰ **What is this bank's SWIFT code?**
この銀行の国際識別コードは？
Kono ginkō no kokusai shikibetsu kōdo wa?

# At the Post Office

MP3

13_03

① **Can I open a savings account here?**

預金口座の開設は、この窓口でいいんですか？

Yokin-kōza no kaisetsu wa, kono madoguchi de ii n' desu ka?

② **How long will this take by express mail?**

速達で何日かかりますか？

Sokutatsu de nannichi kakarimasu ka?

③ **I need a return receipt on this.**

これ、配達証明付きにしてください。

Kore, haitatsu-shōmei-tsuki ni shite kudasai.

④ **Is this guaranteed to arrive by tomorrow?**

これ、必ず明日じゅうに着きますか？

Kore, kanarazu asujū ni tsukimasu ka?

⑤ **I need to send this small packet to London.**

この小包をロンドンに送りたいんですけど。

Kono kozutsumi o Rondon ni okuritai n' desu kedo.

⑥ **How much will it cost to send this EMS?**

これをEMSで送ると、いくらかかりますか？

Kore o ī-emu-esu de okuru to, ikura kakarimasu ka?

⑦ **I need to insure this package.**

この小包、書留でお願いします。

Kono kozutsumi, kakitome de onegai shimasu.

⑧ **I want this to get there as fast as possible.**

できるだけ早く届く方法で送りたいんですけど。

Dekiru dake hayaku todoku hōhō de okuritai n' desu kedo.

---

⑨ **I'm here to pick up a missed delivery.**

不在郵便を受け取りに来ました。

Fuzai-yūbin o uketori ni kimashita.

---

⑩ **Do you have prepaid postcards here?**

官製はがきは置いてありますか？

Kansei hagaki wa oite arimasu ka?

---

# By Courier

MP3
13_04

① **What's the maximum size box I can send?**

宅配便で送れる最大のサイズは？

Takuhaibin de okureru saidai no saizu wa?

---

② **Can I send a box that weighs 30 kilograms?**

重さ30キロの荷物は、
宅配便で送れますか？

Omosa sanjukkiro no nimotsu wa,
takuhaibin de okuremasu ka?

---

③ **Can I send this package COD?**

この荷物、代引きで送れますか？

Kono nimotsu, daibiki de okuremasu ka?

④ **I need it delivered between two and four P.M.**

午後2時から4時の指定でお願いします。

Gogo niji kara yoji no shitei de onegai shimasu.

⑤ **I'm calling about a delivery I missed.**

不在票がはいっていたので、お電話しました。

Fuzaihyō ga haitteita no de, o-denwa shimashita.

⑥ **Can you redeliver the package tonight?**

今夜、再配達してもらえますか？

Kon'ya, saihaitatsu shite moraemasu ka?

⑦ **I sent the document by motorcycle courier.**

書類をバイク便で送りました。

Shorui o baikubin de okurimashita.

⑧ **Let's send our skis ahead to the airport.**

スキー板だけ、先に宅配便で空港へ送っておこうよ。

Sukī-ita dake, saki ni takuhaibin de kūkō e okutte okō yo.

⑨ **Is it safer to send this by refrigerated truck?**

これ、クール便にしたほうが安全ですか？

Kore, kūrubin ni shita hō ga anzen desu ka?

# Getting Phones and Phone Lines

13_05

① **We need two separate lines installed.**

電話回線を2本引きたいんですけど。

Denwa-kaisen o nihon hikitai n' desu kedo.

② **We'd like to have a phone jack in each room.**

各部屋に電話用のモジュラー・ジャックが

ほしいです。

Kaku heya ni denwa-yō no mojurā-jakku ga
hoshii desu.

③ **I want just a plain old phone, no bells and whistles.**

よけいな機能なんか付いてない、

ごくシンプルな電話機がほしいんです。

Yokei na kinō nanka tsuite 'nai,
goku shimpuru na denwaki ga hoshii n' desu.

④ **What's the down payment for a landline?**

固定電話の加入には、いくらかかりますか？

Kotei-denwa no kanyū ni wa, ikura kakarimasu ka?

⑤ **I'd like to see your newest cell phones.**

携帯の最新機種を見せてください。

Keitai no saishin-kishu o misete kudasai.

⑥ **What are the special features of this model?**

この機種の特徴は何ですか？

Kono kishu no tokuchō wa nan desu ka?

⑦ **My biggest concern is battery life.**

いちばん重視したいのは、電池の持続時間です。

Ichiban jūshi shitai no wa, denchi no jizoku-jikan desu.

⑧ **How do I change the answering mode?**

留守電のモード切替は、どうやるんですか？

Rusuden no mōdo-kirikae wa, dō yaru n' desu ka?

## Accessing Internet and E-mail

MP3
13_06

① **I want your cheapest Internet setup plan.**

いちばん安いセットアップ・プランで
お願いします。

Ichiban yasui settoappu-puran de
onegai shimasu.

② **How fast is the connection?**

通信速度は、どのくらいですか？

Tsūshin-sokudo wa, dono kurai desu ka?

③ **What are your monthly all-inclusive charges?**

ぜんぶ込みで、毎月の料金はいくらですか？

Zembu komi de, maitsuki no ryōkin wa ikura desu ka?

④ **Do you offer support in English?**

英語のサポートは、ありますか？

Eigo no sapōto wa, arimasu ka?

⑤ **How good are your spam filters?**

スパム・フィルターの性能は、どのくらいですか？

Supamu-firutā no seinō wa, dono kurai desu ka?

⑧ **What can I do to protect against viruses?**

ウイルス対策は、何ができますか？

Uirusu-taisaku wa, nani ga dekimasu ka?

---

# Making Business Cards

**MP3**
13_07

① **I need a bilingual, double-sided card.**

片面は英語、片面は日本語の名刺を
作りたいんですが。

Katamen wa Eigo, katamen wa Nihongo no meishi o
tsukuritai n' desu ga.

---

② **Do you have any thicker card stock?**

もう少し厚手の紙、ありますか？

Mō sukoshi atsude no kami, arimasu ka?

---

③ **Let me see your book of fonts and ink colors.**

書体と文字色の見本を見せてください。

Shotai to mojiiro no mihon o misete kudasai.

---

④ **Do you have a closely matching Japanese font?**

これとよく似た和文書体は、ありますか？

Kore to yoku nita wabun-shotai wa, arimasu ka?

---

⑤ **I'd like a single-sided card with a printed logo.**

ロゴ入りで片面印刷の名刺を作りたいんですが。

Rogo-iri de katamen-insatsu no meishi o tsukuritai n' desu ga.

⑥ **Can you add my photo to this upper-left corner?**

この左上の隅に顔写真を入れられますか？

Kono hidariue no sumi ni kaojashin o ireraremasu ka?

⑦ **I don't like this shiny-coated paper so much.**

こういう光沢のある紙は、
あまり好きじゃありません。

Kō iu kōtaku no aru kami wa,
amari suki ja arimasen.

⑧ **I want this same card but with a new address.**

住所だけ差し替えて、同じ名刺を刷ってください。

Jūsho dake sashikaete, onaji meishi o sutte kudasai.

⑨ **How fast can you print up 500 of these?**

この名刺500枚だと、最短で、いつできますか？

Kono meishi gohyakumai da to, saitan de, itsu dekimasu ka?

# Getting Repairs

MP3

13_08

① **My computer keeps crashing for no reason.**

うちのコンピューター、なぜか、
やたら故障するんです。

Uchi no kompyūtā, nazeka,
yatara koshō suru n' desu.

② **Can you replace the heels on these boots?**

このブーツ、ヒールを付け替えてもらえますか?

Kono būtsu, hīru o tsukekaete moraemasu ka?

③ **My refrigerator is making a strange noise.**

うちの冷蔵庫、変な音がするんです。

Uchi no reizōko, hen na oto ga suru n' desu.

④ **Is it possible to fix this?**

これ、直せますか?

Kore, naosemasu ka?

⑤ **Can you repair the handle on my bag?**

このバッグの持ち手、修理できますか?

Kono baggu no mochite, shūri dekimasu ka?

⑥ **When can I get it back?**

いつごろ、修理、できあがりますか?

Itsugoro, shūri, dekiagarimasu ka?

⑦ **Can you service my car by tomorrow?**

車の修理、あすじゅうに、できますか?

Kuruma no shūri, asujū ni dekimasu ka?

⑧ **Do I need to change the batteries?**

電池を交換しないとダメですか?

Denchi o kōkan shinai to dame desu ka?

⑨ **When I turn it on, nothing happens.**

電源をオンにしても、何も反応しないんです。

Dengen o on ni shite mo, nanimo hannō shinai n' desu.

⑩ **Something's wrong with the motor, I think.**
モーターの故障じゃないかと思うんですけど。
Mōtā no koshō ja nai ka to omou n' desu kedo.

⑪ **Can you give me an estimate on repairs?**
修理の見積りを出していただけますか？
Shūri no mitsumori o dashite itadakemasu ka?

# Media Access

MP3
13_09

① **I'd like to subscribe to your paper.**
新聞の購読を申し込みたいんですけど。
Shimbun no kōdoku o mōshikomitai n' desu kedo.

② **My newspaper didn't come today.**
けさの朝刊が来てません。
Kesa no chōkan ga kite 'masen.

③ **I'll be away, so please cancel my paper delivery for two weeks.**
2週間ほど留守にしますので、
配達を止めてください。
Nishūkan hodo rusu ni shimasu no de,
haitatsu o tomete kudasai.

④ **I'd like to know how to get CNN at home.**
うちでCNNを見るには、どうすればいいですか？
Uchi de shī-enu-enu o miru ni wa, dōsureba ii desu ka?

⑤ **How do I sign up to get that newsletter?**

そのニューズレターの購読は、
どうやって申し込むんですか？

Sono nyūzuretā no kōdoku wa,
dō yatte mōshikomu n' desu ka?

⑥ **I'd like to put an ad in your paper.**

おたくの新聞に広告を出したいんですが。

Otaku no shimbun ni kōkoku o dashitai n' desu ga.

⑦ **Where can I find free magazines in English?**

英語のフリー・マガジンって、
どこに行けば置いてあるの？

Eigo no furīmagajin tte,
doko ni ikeba oite aru no?

⑧ **Send me the link.**

リンク、送って。

Rinku, okutte.

MP3

13_10

# Dealing with Documents

① **I need to update my alien registration card.**

外国人登録証、更新しなくちゃ。

Gaikokujin-tōrokushō, kōshin shinakucha.

② **I have to stop in at the U.S. Embassy.**

アメリカ大使館に寄る用事があるんです。

Amerika Taishikan ni yoru yōji ga aru n' desu.

③ **I need a copy of my work contract for Immigration.**

入国管理局に提出するので、
労働契約書のコピーをください。

Nyūkoku-kanrikyoku ni teishutsu suru no de,

rōdōkeiyakusho no kopī o kudasai.

④ **I need to renew my re-entry permit.**

再入国許可証、更新しなくちゃ。

Sainyūkoku-kyokashō, kōshin shinakucha.

⑤ **I need to get a birth certificate for our new baby.**

赤ちゃんが生まれたので、
出生証明書を取りにいかないと。

Akachan ga umareta no de,

shussei-shōmeisho o torini ikanai to.

⑥ **To work, do I need to change my visa status?**

就労する場合は、ビザの在留資格変更が
必要ですか？

Shūrō suru baai wa, biza no zairyū-shikaku henkō ga

hitsuyō desu ka?

⑦ **What's the easiest way to extend my visa?**

ビザの在留期間を延長するには、
どういう方法がいちばん簡単ですか？

Biza no zairyū-kikan o enchō suru ni wa,
dō iu hōhō ga ichiban kantan desu ka?

⑧ **I need a document proving I paid my taxes.**

納税証明書を発行してください。

Nōzei-shōmeisho o hakkō shite kudasai.

⑨ **How do I apply for a Japanese driver's license?**

免許証って、どうやって申請するの？

Menkyoshō tte, dō yatte shinsei suru no?

⑩ **Will this card suffice as personal identification?**

このカード、身分証明になりますか？

Kono kādo, mibun-shōmei ni narimasu ka?

⑪ **Here are my expenses and itemized receipts.**

これが経費と領収明細書です。

Kore ga keihi to ryōshū-meisaisho desu.

## Doctor's Office

MP3
14_01

① **I need a general physical checkup.**
人間ドックをお願いします。
Ningen-dokku o onegai shimasu.

② **I feel serious pain right here.**
ここに強い痛みがあるんです。
Koko ni tsuyoi itami ga aru n' desu.

③ **Can you take a look at this rash?**
この発疹を診ていただきたいんです。
Kono hosshin o mite itadakitai n' desu.

④ **I threw up and had diarrhea all day yesterday.**
きのう一日じゅう、嘔吐と下痢が続きました。
Kinō ichinichijū, ōto to geri ga tsuzukimashita.

⑤ **I need to be seen as soon as possible.**
できるだけ早く診察してください。
Dekiru dake hayaku shinsatsu shite kudasai.

⑥ **I have a fever and chills.**
熱があって、寒気がします。
Netsu ga atte, samuke ga shimasu.

⑦ **I have a mild, persistent ache right here.**

ここのところに弱い痛みがずっと
続いているんです。

Koko no tokoro ni yowai itami ga zutto
tsuzuite iru n' desu.

---

⑧ **I can't sleep and I feel exhausted all the time.**

眠れなくて、いつも疲れてる感じなんです。

Nemurenakute, itsumo tsukarete 'ru kanji nan desu.

---

⑨ **I'm congested and dizzy, but I don't have a cough.**

鼻が詰まって、めまいがしますが、
咳は出ません。

Hana ga tsumatte, memai ga shimasu ga,
seki wa demasen.

---

## Medications

MP3
14_02

① **I'd like to get more of this cough suppressant.** (speaking to a doctor)

この咳止めを、もう少し出して
いただけますか？

Kono sekidome o, mō sukoshi dashite
itadakemasu ka?

**②   Is it best to take this medication after or before a meal?**

この薬は、食前ですか？　食後ですか？

Kono kusuri wa, shokuzen desu ka? Shokugo desu ka?

---

**③   What is the name of this antibiotic?**

この抗生物質は、何という名前の薬ですか？

Kono kōsei-busshitsu wa, nan to iu namae no kusuri desu ka?

---

**④   How often should I apply this ointment?**

この軟膏は、一日何回付けるんですか？

Kono nankō wa, ichinichi nankai tsukeru n' desu ka?

Health and Beauty

---

**⑤   Will this medication make me drowsy?**

この薬は、眠くなりますか？

Kono kusuri wa, nemuku narimasu ka?

---

**⑥   I'm allergic to penicillin, so I can't take this.**

わたしはペニシリン・アレルギーなので、
この薬はだめなんです。

Watashi wa penishirin-arerugī na no de,
kono kusuri wa dame nan desu.

---

**⑦   Is there anything I can't eat or drink with this medication?**

この薬を服用中に飲んだり食べたりして
いけないものは、ありますか？

Kono kusuri o fukuyōchū ni nondari tabetari shite
ikenai mono wa, arimasu ka?

⑧ **Are there any side effects from these meds?**

この薬は、副作用がありますか?

Kono kusuri wa, fukusayō ga arimasu ka?

---

## Conditions and Symptoms

**MP3**
14_03

① **I have pretty bad constipation.**

わたし、便秘がひどくて……。

Watashi, bempi ga hidokute . . .

② **The doctor said my liver is shot!**

医者から、肝臓がボロボロですよ、って
言われちゃった!

Isha kara, kanzō ga boroboro desu yo tte
iwarechatta!

③ **I suffer from kidney stones.**

わたし、腎臓結石があるんです。

Watashi, jinzō-kesseki ga aru n' desu.

④ **Two people in my family have had appendicitis.**

家族のうち、二人が虫垂炎をやっています。

Kazoku no uchi, futari ga chūsuien o yatte imasu.

⑤ **My lungs are damaged from smoking.**

タバコのせいで、肺が悪くなってるんです。

Tabako no sei de, hai ga waruku natte 'ru n' desu.

⑥ **That food really upsets my stomach.**

それを食べると、てきめんに、

おなかをこわすんです。

Sore o taberu to, tekimen ni,
onaka o kowasu n' desu.

⑦ **I'm having trouble performing in bed.**

夜の生活がうまくいかないんです。

Yoru no seikatsu ga umaku ikanai n' desu.

⑧ **I get very serious cramps during menstruation.**

生理痛がとてもひどいんです。

Seiritsū ga totemo hidoi n' desu.

⑨ **Lately I've been troubled by IBS.**

このところ、過敏性大腸炎で苦しんでいます。

Konotokoro, kabinsei-daichōen de kurushinde imasu.

⑩ **I'm having symptoms of heart trouble.**

心臓病の症状があるんです。

Shinzōbyō no shōjō ga aru n' desu.

# Dentist, Orthodontist, Optometrist

MP3
14_04

① **I'd like a cleaning and a checkup.**

歯のクリーニングとチェックをお願いします。

Ha no kurīningu to chekku o onegai shimasu.

**②　My upper molar is sensitive to cold drinks.**

冷たいものを飲むと、上の奥歯がしみるんです。

Tsumetai mono o nomu to, ue no okuba ga shimiru n' desu.

---

**③　Please give me something to numb the pain.**

麻酔を使ってください。

Masui o tsukatte kudasai.

---

**④　Can you just provide a temporary crown?**

とりあえず、仮歯だけ入れてもらえますか？

Toriaezu, kariba dake irete moraemasu ka?

---

**⑤　How many visits will this require?**

治療に何回くらいかかりますか？

Chiryō ni nankai kurai kakarimasu ka?

---

**⑥　Is this covered by my health insurance?**

この治療は保険がききますか？

Kono chiryō wa hoken ga kikimasu ka?

---

**⑦　How much would it cost to straighten my teeth?**

歯の矯正は、どのくらい費用がかかりますか？

Ha no kyōsei wa, dono kurai hiyō ga kakarimasu ka?

---

**⑧　I need my eyes tested.**

視力を測ってもらえますか？

Shiryoku o hakatte moraemasu ka?

---

**⑨　There's something stuck in my eye.**

目に何かはいってるみたいなんですけど。

Me ni nanika haitte 'ru mitai nan desu kedo.

⑩ **Would you recommend LASIK or just glasses?**

レーシックがいいでしょうか？
それとも、眼鏡でいいですか？

Rēshikku ga ii deshō ka?
Sore tomo, megane de ii desu ka?

# Exercise

MP3
14_05

① **My favorite workout is a long run, then a swim.**

トレーニングなら、長距離走のあと水泳、って
メニューが好きです。

Torēningu nara, chōkyorisō no ato suiei tte
menyū ga suki desu.

② **I almost never work out. I'm a couch potato.**

わたし、運動はほとんどしません。
カウチ・ポテト族ですから。

Watashi, undō wa hotondo shimasen.
Kauchipoteto-zoku desu kara.

③ **Like they say, no pain, no gain!**

苦労なければ成果なし、って言うでしょ！

Kurō nakereba seika nashi tte iu desho!

**④ My trainer has me lifting heavy weights every day.**

トレーナーに言われて、
毎日かなり重いウエイトを上げています。

Torēnā ni iwarete,

mainichi kanari omoi ueito o agete imasu.

---

**⑤ Wow, your gym time is really paying off!**

F　あら、ジム通いの成果が出てきたじゃない！

　Ara, jimu-gayoi no seika ga detekita ja nai!

M　おっ、ジム通いの成果が出てきたね！

　O, jimu-gayoi no seika ga detekita ne!

---

**⑥ I pulled a muscle, and that's made me lazy.**

肉離れをやったせいで、
動きにキレがなくなったんです。

Nikubanare o yatta sei de,

ugoki ni kire ga nakunatta n' desu.

---

**⑦ I dropped five kilos doing Pilates and yoga.**

ピラティスとヨガで、体重が5キロ
落ちたんですよ。

Piratisu to yoga de, taijū ga gokiro

ochita n' desu yo.

⑧ **I get all the exercise I need walking to work.**

会社まで歩いて通うだけで、運動は足りてるよ。

Kaisha made aruite kayou dake de, undō wa tarite 'ru yo.

---

## Barber and Salon

MP3
14_06

① **Just trim a little off the sides.**

サイドをそろえる程度に、
少しだけ切ってください。

Saido o soroeru teido ni,
sukoshi dake kitte kudasai.

② **Can you just follow my current style?**

いまの髪型と
同じ感じにしてください。

Ima no kamigata to
onaji kanji ni shite kudasai.

③ **I want a cut that makes me look younger.**

若く見えるカットにしてください。

Wakaku mieru katto ni shite kudasai.

④ **Can you color my hair without damaging it?**

髪を傷めないヘアカラーは、ありますか?

Kami o itamenai heakarā wa, arimasu ka?

⑤ **I hate the way my hair does this!**

M ぼくの髪、こうなっちゃうから、いやなんだよな！

Boku no kami, kō natchau kara, iya nan da yo na!

F わたしの髪、こうなっちゃうから、いやなのよね！

Watashi no kami, kō natchau kara, iya na no yo ne!

⑥ **I'd like a perm.**

パーマ、お願いします。

Pāma, onegai shimasu.

⑦ **Can you style my hair like in this photo?**

この写真みたいなスタイルにできますか？

Kono shashin mitai na sutairu ni dekimasu ka?

⑧ **Can you give me some subtle highlights?**

おとなしい感じのハイライト、入れてもらえますか？

Otonashii kanji no hairaito, irete moraemasu ka?

⑨ **I want a totally low-maintenance cut.**

とにかく手入れの楽なスタイルに

カットしてください。

Tonikaku te-ire no raku na sutairu ni
katto shite kudasai.

⑩ **Can I get a shave and eyebrow trim?**

顔そりと眉カットをお願いできますか？

Kaosori to mayukatto o onegai dekimasu ka?

# Esthetic Treatments and Cosmetic Surgery

**MP3**
14_07

① **I'd like to come in for a consultation.**

カウンセリングをお願いしたいんですけど。

Kaunseringu o onegai shitai n' desu kedo.

② **I'd like a smaller nose and to erase these moles.**

鼻をもう少し小さくして、
このへんのほくろを取りたいです。

Hana o mō sukoshi chiisaku shite,
kono hen no hokuro o toritai desu.

③ **Book me for a bikini wax and manicure.**

ビキニラインの脱毛とネイルケアで、
予約をお願いします。

Bikinirain no datsumō to neirukea de,
yoyaku o onegai shimasu.

④ **Can I get a massage and facial today?**

きょうは、マッサージとフェイシャルを
お願いできますか？

Kyō wa, massāji to feisharu o
onegai dekimasu ka?

⑤ **I want to slim down my thighs and waist.**

ふともも と ウエスト を細<sub>ほそ</sub>くしたいです。

Futomomo to uesuto o hosoku shitai desu.

⑥ **I'd love to try reflexology, but does it hurt?**

リフレクソロジーを試<sub>ため</sub>してみたいけど、
痛<sub>いた</sub>くないですか？

Rifurekusorojī o tameshite mitai kedo,
itakunai desu ka?

⑦ **How long will it take to recover from this?**

腫れが引<sub>ひ</sub>くまでに、何日<sub>なんにち</sub>ぐらいかかりますか？

Hare ga hiku made ni, nannichi gurai kakarimasu ka?

⑧ **I'd like to try laser hair removal.**

レーザー脱毛<sub>だつもう</sub>を試<sub>ため</sub>してみたいです。

Rēzā-datsumō o tameshite mitai desu.

⑨ **I want to enhance this part, and get rid of this.**

ここをもっと強調<sub>きょうちょう</sub>して、こっちを取<sub>と</sub>りたいです。

Koko o motto kyōchō shite, kotchi o toritai desu.

⑩ **How long will these results last?**

効果<sub>こうか</sub>は、どのくらいもちますか？

Kōka wa, dono kurai mochimasu ka?

# Self-assessment

**MP3**
**14_08**

① **I hate my thighs!**

F わたし、このふとももが、いやなのよね！
Watashi, kono futomomo ga iya na no yo ne!

② **I really need to do something about my arms.**
この腕、ほんと、何とかしないと……。
Kono ude, honto, nantoka shinai to . . .

③ **My eyes are my best feature.**
自分の顔で一番好きなところは、目です。
Jibun no kao de ichiban suki na tokoro wa me desu.

④ **I can't help being heavy. It's in my genes.**
太めの体形はしかたないよ、遺伝だから。
Futome no taikei wa shikatanai yo, iden da kara.

⑤ **I was born with bad skin.**
生まれつき、肌が弱いんです。
Umaretsuki, hada ga yowai n' desu.

⑥ **I'm sorta getting a beer belly here.**
ちょっとビール腹になりかけてるなぁ。
Chotto bīrubara ni narikakete 'ru nā.

⑦ **I'm hoping to lose a few this year.**
今年は少しやせたいな。
Kotoshi wa sukoshi yasetai na.

⑧ **I'm in pretty good shape, if you ask me.**

言っちゃなんですけど、
スタイルには自信あるんですよ。

Itcha nan' desu kedo,
sutairu ni wa jishin aru n' desu yo.

# Diet and Reactions to Food

MP3
14_09

① **I'm a very strict vegetarian.**

わたしは厳格なベジタリアンです。

Watashi wa genkaku na bejitarian desu.

② **That looks delicious, but I'm on a diet.**

おいしそうだけど、わたし、ダイエット中だから。

Oishisō da kedo, watashi, daiettochū da kara.

③ **I have Celiac disease, so gluten is out for me.**

わたしはセリアック病なので、

グルテンはダメなんです。

Watashi wa Seriakkubyō na no de,
guruten wa dame nan desu.

④ **I can eat almost anything except raw fish.**

お刺身以外なら、ほとんど何でも食べられます。

O-sashimi igai nara, hotondo nandemo taberaremasu.

⑤ **If I eat fried foods, I get really bad heartburn.**

揚げ物を食べると、ひどい胸焼けがするんです。

Agemono o taberu to, hidoi muneyake ga suru n' desu.

---

⑥ **I love tomatoes, but they don't agree with me.**

トマトは好きだけど、体質的に合わないんです。

Tomato wa suki da kedo, taishitsuteki ni awanai n' desu.

---

⑦ **The last time I ate clams, I got sick.**

このまえハマグリを食べたら、
ぐあい悪くなって吐いちゃった。

Konomae hamaguri o tabetara,
guai waruku natte haichatta.

---

⑧ **I have to follow a low-sodium, low-fat diet.**

食塩と脂肪の摂取制限があるんです。

Shokuen to shibō no sesshu-seigen ga aru n' desu.

---

⑨ **I'm deathly allergic to peanuts.**

ピーナッツを食べると、命にかかわる重度の
アレルギーが出ます。

Pīnattsu o taberu to, inochi ni kakawaru jūdo no
arerugī ga demasu.

# Special Circumstances

① **I carry an inhaler for my asthma.**
喘息なので、吸入器を持ち歩いています。
Zensoku na no de, kyūnyūki o mochiaruite imasu.

② **My arthritis is killing me today.**
きょうは、関節炎の痛みがとくにひどいなぁ……。
Kyō wa, kansetsuen no itami ga tokuni hidoi nā . . .

③ **I can't ski because I have a bum knee.**
膝を壊しちゃって、もう、スキーはできないんだ。
Hiza o kowashichatte, mō, sukī wa dekinai n' da.

④ **He has a limp from a childhood accident.**
彼は、子供のころの事故が原因で、
足をひきずって歩くんです。
Kare wa, kodomo no koro no jiko ga gen'in de,
ashi o hikizutte aruku n' desu.

⑤ **She suffers from severe osteoporosis.**
彼女は、深刻な骨粗しょう症になっています。
Kanojo wa, shinkoku na kotsusoshōshō ni natte imasu.

⑥ **He lost his eyesight as a baby.**
彼は、赤ん坊のころに視力を失いました。
Kare wa, akambō no koro ni shiryoku o ushinaimashita.

⑦ **She's losing her hearing.**
彼女、耳が遠くなってきたね。
Kanojo, mimi ga tōku natte kita ne.

⑧ **This injury is from a bad car accident.**
この傷は、ひどい交通事故が原因です。
Kono kizu wa, hidoi kōtsūjiko ga gen'in desu.

⑨ **I'm still fighting the cancer, but I'm going to win!**
現在も癌で闘病中ですが、
きっと克服してみせます！
Genzai mo gan de tōbyōchū desu ga,
kitto kokufuku shite misemasu!

> **Chapter**
> **15**

# The Private Zone

## Getting Started or Stalled

**15_01**

① **Are you with someone?**

ひとり？　だれかと来たの？

Hitori? Dareka to kita no?

② **I couldn't help noticing you.**

F あなたみたいな人が目にはいらないはず、

ないでしょ。

Anata mitai na hito ga me ni hairanai hazu, nai desho.

M きみみたいな人が目にはいらないはず、ないよ。

Kimi mitai na hito ga me ni hairanai hazu, nai yo.

③ **Want to get together sometime?**

こんど、どこかで会わない？

Kondo, dokoka de awanai?

④ **Are you doing anything later?**

このあと、何か予定あるの？

Kono ato, nanika yotei aru no?

⑤ **Are you hitting on me?**

それって、ナンパしてるわけ？

Sore tte, nampa shite 'ru wake?

⑥ **Can I sit next to you?**

となり、座ってもいい？

Tonari, suwatte mo ii?

⑦ **Can I get you something from the bar?**

何か飲む？

Nanika, nomu?

⑧ **Care to dance?**

ダンスしない？

Dansu shinai?

⑨ **Not tonight.**

M 今夜は、だめなんだ。

Kon'ya wa, dame nan da.

F 今夜は、だめなの。

Kon'ya wa, dame na no.

⑩ **I'm waiting for someone.**

人を待ってるから。

Hito o matte 'ru kara.

⑪ **I swing the other way.**

M ぼく、女には興味ないんだ……。

Boku, onna ni wa kyōmi nai n' da . . .

F わたし、男には興味ないの……。

Watashi, otoko ni wa kyōmi nai no . . .

The Private Zone

⑫ **Maybe some other time.**

また、いつか。

Mata, itsuka.

---

# Sweet Talk

MP3
15_02

① **You look fabulous.**

M すっごいステキだよ。

Suggoi suteki da yo.

F すっごくステキよ。

Suggoku suteki yo.

---

② **You're a great dancer.**

ダンス、うまいね。

Dansu, umai ne.

---

③ **You're beautiful.**

美人だね。

Bijin da ne.

---

④ **I'm having a great time with you.**

F 一緒にいると、すごく楽しいわ。

Issho ni iru to, sugoku tanoshii wa.

M 一緒にいると、すごく楽しいよ。

Issho ni iru to, sugoku tanoshii yo.

⑤　**I've never met someone like you before.**

M　きみみたいな人は、初めてだな……。
Kimi mitai na hito wa, hajimete da na . . .

F　あなたみたいな人、初めてだわ……。
Anata mitai na hito, hajimete da wa . . .

⑥　**I like the way you handle things.**

F　頼りになるところが、すてきよ。
Tayori ni naru tokoro ga, suteki yo.

M　頼りになるところが、すてきだよ。
Tayori ni naru tokoro ga, suteki da yo.

⑦　**You have gorgeous eyes.**

M　きみの瞳は、すごく魅力的だ。
Kimi no hitomi wa, sugoku miryokuteki da.

F　あなたの瞳、とっても魅力的……。
Anata no hitomi, tottemo miryokuteki . . .

⑧　**You light up the room.**

F　あなたがいると、まわりが明るくなるわ。
Anata ga iru to, mawari ga akaruku naru wa.

M　きみがいると、まわりが明るくなるよ。
Kimi ga iru to, mawari ga akaruku naru yo.

The Private Zone

⑨ **You're incredibly sharp.**

めっちゃアタマいいんだね。

Metcha atama ii n' da ne.

---

# Going Out

MP3
15_03

① **What kind of food do you like?**

食べ物は、何が好き？

Tabemono wa, nani ga suki?

② **Do you want to do something different tonight?**

今夜は、ちょっとちがうこと、してみる？

Kon'ya wa, chotto chigau koto, shite miru?

③ **Can I pick you up at about seven?**

7時ごろ迎えに行くけど、いい？

Shichiji goro mukaeniiku kedo, ii?

④ **How should I dress?**

どんな服で行けばいい？

Donna fuku de ikeba ii?

⑤ **Will it be just the two of us?**

わたしたち二人だけ？

Watashitachi futari dake?

⑥ **Let's go someplace where we can talk privately.**

二人きりで話せる場所へ行こう……。

Futarikiri de hanaseru basho e ikō . . .

⑦ **Are we exclusive?**

ほかの人とは、もう付き合わないことにする？

Hoka no hito to wa, mō tsukiawanai koto ni suru?

---

⑧ **Are you going out with anyone else?**

だれか、ほかに付き合ってる人、いる？

Dareka, hoka ni tsukiatte 'ru hito, iru?

---

⑨ **Are we getting serious here?**

これって、本気になりかけてるのかな……？

Kore tte, honki ni narikakete 'ru no ka na . . . ?

---

⑩ **I'd definitely like to see more of you.**

もっと会いたいよ。

Motto aitai yo.

---

## Moving Forward

MP3
15_04

① **Can I walk you home?**

家まで送ろうか？

Ie made okurō ka?

---

② **Do you want to come in?**

上がっていく？

Agatte iku?

---

③ **Can I take you somewhere private?**

どっか、二人きりになれるところへ行かない？

Dokka, futarikiri ni nareru tokoro e ikanai?

④ **Is there a love hotel near here?**

近くにラブ・ホテル、あるかな？

Chikaku ni rabuhoteru, aru ka na?

---

⑤ **I really want you.**

M きみがほしいよ。

Kimi ga hoshii yo.

F あなたがほしい……。

Anata ga hoshii . . .

---

⑥ **I'm so ready, are you?**

F わたしは、いますぐでも……。あなたは？

Watashi wa, ima sugu demo . . . Anata wa?

M ぼくは、いますぐでも……。きみは？

Boku wa, ima sugu demo . . . Kimi wa?

---

⑦ **You wanna do it?**

ね、エッチしない？

Ne, etchi shinai?

---

⑧ **I'm not so sure about this, but . . .**

まだ、ちょっと迷ってるんだけど……。

Mada, chotto mayotte 'ru n' da kedo . . .

---

⑨ **This is going too fast for me.**

ちょっと展開が速すぎて……。

Chotto tenkai ga hayasugite . . .

⑩ **I'm on fire.**

もう、がまんできないよ……。

Mō, gaman dekinai yo . . .

---

# Getting Into It

MP3
15_05

① **Are you okay with this?**

いい？

Ii?

② **Do you have protection?**

コンドーム、ある？

Kondōmu, aru?

③ **Are you using birth control?**

ピル、飲んでる？

Piru, nonde 'ru?

④ **I have my period.**

いま、生理なの。

Ima, seiri na no.

⑤ **Do you mind if I do this?**

これ、いやじゃない？

Kore, iya ja nai?

⑥ **I don't like doing that.**

それ、好きじゃない……。

Sore, suki ja nai . . .

⑦ **Harder please.**

もっと強くして……。

Motto tsuyoku shite . . .

⑧ **Give me your hand and I'll show you.**

手、貸して……。こうやって……。

Te, kashite . . . Kō yatte . . .

⑨ **Can I kiss you here?**

ここにキスしてもいい？

Koko ni kisu shite mo ii?

⑩ **Yes, that's it!**

そう……そう！

Sō . . . sō!

⑪ **I think we'd better stop now.**

ねえ、もう、やめとこうよ……。

Nē, mō, yametokō yo . . .

⑫ **I have to get home.**

帰らなくちゃ。

Kaeranakucha.

## Climax and Pillow Talk

MP3
15_06

① **Don't stop!**

このまま続けて。

Konomama tsuzukete.

② **I'm so close.**

いきそう……。

Ikisō . . .

③ **Just a little longer.**

もう少し。

Mō sukoshi.

④ **Can I come now?**

いってもいい？

Itte mo ii?

⑤ **I can't stop.**

もう止まらないよ。

Mō tomaranai yo.

⑥ **Don't move.**

動かないで。

Ugokanaide.

⑦ **That was amazing.**

すごくよかったよ。

Sugoku yokatta yo.

⑧ **Let me catch my breath.**

息、つかせて……。

Iki, tsukasete . . .

⑨ **Let me just hold you for a while.**

しばらく、こうやって抱いてていい？

Shibaraku, kō yatte daitete ii?

## Commitment

MP3
15_07

① **I love you very much.**

M 愛してるよ、すごく……。
Aishite 'ru yo, sugoku . . .

F 愛してるわ、とっても……。
Aishite 'ru wa, tottemo . . .

② **We've been going out for a long time.**
付き合いはじめて、もう、ずいぶんになるよね。
Tsukiaihajimete, mō, zuibun ni naru yo ne.

③ **I want this to be just the two of us.**
これからは、一対一で付き合いたいな。
Kore kara wa, ittai-ichi de tsukiaitai na.

④ **Do you think we should move in together?**
一緒に住もうか？
Issho ni sumō ka?

⑤ **I'd like us to be even closer.**
もっと、一緒にいたいね。
Motto, issho ni itai ne.

⑥ **I can really see a future for us.**
ずっと二人でやっていけそうな気がするよ。
Zutto futari de yatte ikesō na ki ga suru yo.

⑦ **Are you thinking about marriage at all?**

結婚とか、考えたりする？

Kekkon to ka, kangaetari suru?

⑧ **I'm not ready to make any promises yet.**

F まだ、将来を約束するのは早いような
気がするの。

Mada shōrai o yakusoku suru no wa hayai yō na
ki ga suru no.

M まだ、将来を約束するのは早いような
気がするんだ。

Mada shōrai o yakusoku suru no wa hayai yō na
ki ga suru n' da.

⑨ **I'd like to keep our relationship open for now.**

M いまはまだ、縛られない関係でいたいんだ。

Ima wa mada, shibararenai kankei de itai n' da.

F いまはまだ、縛られない関係でいたいの。

Ima wa mada, shibararenai kankei de itai no.

⑩ **I love you, but I can't see us together forever.**

愛してるけど、先のことまでは、

わからないよ……。

Aishite 'ru kedo, saki no koto made wa,
wakaranai yo. . .

The Private Zone

⑪ **I'm not ready to start a family and all that.**

結婚とか家庭とか、まだ考えられないな。

Kekkon to ka katei to ka, mada kangaerarenai na.

---

# Clarifications and Complications

**MP3**

**15_08**

---

① **I'm gay.**

ぼく、ゲイなんだ。

Boku, gei nan da.

---

② **I'm a lesbian.**

わたし、レズビアンなの。

Watashi, rezubian na no.

---

③ **I'm bisexual.**

M ぼく、バイセクシャルなんだ。

Boku, baisekusharu nan da.

F わたし、バイセクシャルなの。

Watashi, baisekusharu na no.

---

④ **I can't have children.**

F わたし、子供は産めないの。

Watashi, kodomo wa umenai no.

M ぼく、子供はできないんだ。

Boku, kodomo wa dekinai n' da.

⑤ **I can't get it up.**

勃たないんだ……。

Tatanai n' da . . .

⑥ **I'm a virgin.**

F わたし、処女なの。

Watashi, shojo na no.

M ぼく、童貞なんだ。

Boku, dōtei nan da.

⑦ **I've got an STD.**

M ぼく、性病があるんだ。

Boku, seibyō ga aru n' da.

F わたし、性病があるの。

Watashi, seibyō ga aru no.

The Private Zone

⑧ **I think I'm pregnant.**

妊娠しちゃったみたい。

Ninshin sichatta mitai.

⑨ **I know you're cheating on me.**

M 浮気してるんだろ？　わかってるんだから。

Uwaki shite 'ru n' daro? Wakatte 'ru n' da kara.

F 浮気してるでしょ？　わかってるんだから。

Uwaki shite 'ru desho? Wakatte 'ru n' da kara.

⑩ **How come you never call me?**

どうして、電話くれないの？

Dōshite, denwa kurenai no?

⑪ **I'm just too busy to spend time with you.**

M 忙しくて、会うひまがないんだよ。

Isogashikute, au hima ga nai n' da yo.

F 忙しくて、会うひまがないのよ。

Isogashikute, au hima ga nai no yo.

⑫ **Obviously we're not meant for each other.**

F わたしたち、ダメかな……。

Watashitachi, dame ka na . . .

M ぼくたち、ダメかな……。

Bokutachi, dame ka na . . .

⑬ **My visa is about to expire.**

ビザがもうすぐ切れるんだ。

Biza ga mō sugu kireru n' da.

⑭ **I think I need some space.**

F 少し距離を置きたいの。

Sukoshi kyori o okitai no.

M 少し距離を置きたいんだ。

Sukoshi kyori o okitai n' da.

⑮ **My parents are freaking out about us.**

M うちの親、ぼくたちのこと知って、
パニクってるよ。
Uchi no oya, bokutachi no koto shitte,
panikutteru yo.

F うちの親、わたしたちのこと知って、
パニクってるわよ。
Uchi no oya, watashitachi no koto shitte,
panikutteru wa yo.

⑯ **We come from two different worlds.**

F わたしたち、住む世界が違うのね。
Watashitachi, sumu sekai ga chigau no ne.

M ぼくたち、住む世界が違うんだね。
Bokutachi, sumu sekai ga chigau n' da ne.

# Anger and Apology

MP3
15_09

① **You really don't get it, do you?**

ほんと、わかってないね！
Honto, wakatte 'nai ne!

② **You're a total jerk.**

F あんたなんか、最低の男だわ！
Anta nanka, saitei no otoko da wa!

254

③ **Why did you lie to me?**

なんで、嘘なんかついたの？

Nande uso nanka tsuita no?

④ **What the hell were you thinking?**

ちょっと！ 何、考えてたわけ？

Chotto! Nani, kangaete 'ta wake?

⑤ **I don't want to see your face anymore.**

M おまえの顔なんか、二度と見たくないよ！

Omae no kao nanka, nido to mitakunai yo!

F あんたの顔なんか、二度と見たくないわよ！

Anta no kao nanka, nido to mitakunai wa yo!

⑥ **You have the wrong idea about this.**

そっちの思いちがいだよ。

Sotchi no omoichigai da yo.

⑦ **That was so stupid and I'm really sorry.**

M すごくバカなことをした……。
本当に、ごめん。

Sugoku baka na koto o shita . . .
Hontō ni, gomen.

F すごくバカなこと、したわ……。
本当に、ごめんね。

Sugoku baka na koto, shita wa . . .
Hontō ni, gomen ne.

⑧ **How can I make it up to you?**

どうしたら、仲直りしてくれる？

Dōshitara, nakanaori shite kureru?

⑨ **Please forgive me.**

ごめんね、許して。

Gomen ne, yurushite.

# Kiss 'n' Tell

15_10

① **After we had sex, all she talks about is marriage.**

彼女、いちど寝たら、
もう、結婚結婚ってうるさいんだ。

Kanojo, ichido netara,

mō, kekkon kekkon tte urusai n' da.

② **He's all talk and no action.**

あの男は、口ばっかりよ。

Ano otoko wa, kuchi bakkari yo.

③ **I think about her night and day.**

寝てもさめても彼女のことしか考えられないよ。

Nete mo samete mo kanojo no koto shika kangaerarenai yo.

④ **He's the one.**

彼こそ、わたしが求めていた人だわ。

Kare koso, watashi ga motomete ita hito da wa.

⑤ **She's dynamite in bed.**

彼女、ベッドの中がすごいんだ。

Kanojo, beddo no naka ga sugoi n' da.

⑥ **He's always on the make and can't be trusted.**

彼ったら、女の子のお尻ばっかり追いかけてて、
信用ならないんだから。

Kare ttara, onna-no-ko no oshiri bakkari oikaketete,
shin'yo naranai n' da kara.

⑦ **I dropped him because he's a workaholic.**

彼とは別れたの、だって仕事の虫なんだもの。

Kare to wa wakareta no, datte shigoto no mushi nan da mono.

⑧ **I'm warning you, she's a gold-digger.**

M いいか、よく聞け。あの女は、金目当てなんだぞ。

Ii ka, yoku kike. Ano onna wa, kane meate nan da zo.

F いい？　よく聞いて。あの女は、お金が目当てなのよ。

Ii? Yoku kiite. Ano onna wa, o-kane ga meate na no yo.

⑨ **He looks normal, but turns totally kinky in bed.**

F 彼、見た目はまともなんだけど、
ベッドでは超ヘンタイなの。

Kare, mitame wa matomo nan da kedo,
beddo de wa chō-hentai nano.

# Babies, Kids, and Teens

## Baby Conceptions

MP3
16_01

① **We've got a bun in the oven!**

F 赤ちゃんができたの！

Akachan ga dekita no!

M 子供ができたんだ！

Kodomo ga dekita n' da!

② **What's the best available prenatal vitamin?**

妊娠中に飲むビタミン剤は、どれがいいですか？

Ninshinchū ni nomu bitaminzai wa, dore ga ii desu ka?

③ **Which obstetrician do you recommend?**

産婦人科は、どこがいいと思う？

Sanfujinka wa, doko ga ii to omou?

④ **Do you offer an epidural on request?**

希望すれば、無痛分娩もできますか？

Kibō sureba, mutsūbumben mo dekimasu ka?

⑤ **She's about five months along.**

彼女、いま、妊娠5ヶ月くらいなんです。

Kanojo, ima, ninshin gokagetsu kurai nan desu.

⑥ **We really like this clinic and the midwives who work here.**

このクリニックは、施設も助産婦さんも、
すごくいいと思います。

Kono kurinikku wa, shisetsu mo josampu-san mo,
sugoku ii to omoimasu.

⑦ **Where can I buy a crib?**

新生児用のベッドは、どこで売っていますか？

Shinseiji-yō no beddo wa, doko de utte imasu ka?

⑧ **I'm going to have an amnio test.**

羊水検査を受けることにしたの。

Yōsui-kensa o ukeru koto ni shita no.

⑨ **When is my next sonogram?**

次回の超音波検査は、いつですか？

Jikai no chōompa-kensa wa, itsu desu ka?

⑩ **Can my husband be present at the birth?**

出産に夫が立ち会うことは、できますか？

Shussan ni otto ga tachiau koto wa, dekimasu ka?

# Babies on the Loose

MP3
16_02

① **Can you recommend a good pediatrician?**

どこか、いい小児科を知りませんか？

Dokoka, ii shōnika o shirimasen ka?

② **What vaccinations are required in Japan?**

日本では、どういうワクチンを打つことに
なってますか？

Nihon de wa, dō iu wakuchin o utsu koto ni
natte 'masu ka?

③ **I can only take three months' maternity leave.**

産休は、３ヶ月しかとれないんです。

Sankyū wa, sankagetsu shika torenai n' desu.

④ **Between night feedings and diapers, we're beat!**

夜中のミルクとおむつ替えで、もう、くたくた！

Yonaka no miruku to omutsugae de, mō, kutakuta!

⑤ **I plan to breastfeed for about a year.**

１歳くらいまで、母乳で育てようと思っています。

Issai kurai made, bonyū de sodateyō to omotte imasu.

⑥ **Our baby is finally sleeping through the night.**

うちの子も、やっと朝まで眠ってくれるように
なったよ。

Uchi no ko mo, yatto asa made nemuttekureru yō ni
natta yo.

⑦ **I really need to find a good babysitter.**

いいベビーシッターを探さないと。

Ii bebīshittā o sagasanai to.

⑧ **Can I get there easily with a baby stroller?**

そこ、ベビーカーでも楽に行ける場所ですか？

Soko, bebīkā demo raku ni ikeru basho desu ka?

⑨ **Which formula do you suggest at six months?**

生後6ヶ月の赤ちゃんには、
どの粉ミルクがいいですか？

Seigo rokkagetsu no akachan ni wa,
dono konamiruku ga ii desu ka?

⑩ **Where can we get discount diapers and stuff?**

紙おむつなんかが安いお店、知ってる？

Kamiomutsu nanka ga yasui o-mise, shitte 'ru?

## Playground Debut

16_03

① **Hi, this is my son Paul. What's your name, little boy?**

F こんにちは。この子、ポールっていうの。
あなたのお名前は？

Konnichiwa. Kono ko, Pōru tte iu no.
Anata no o-namae wa?

M こんにちは。この子、ポールっていうんだ。
きみの名前は？

Konnichiwa. Kono ko, Pōru tte iu n' da.
Kimi no namae wa?

② **How old is your little girl? Mine's three.**

お子さんは何歳ですか？　うちの子は3歳です。

Okosan wa nansai desu ka? Uchi no ko wa sansai desu.

③ **Those two really seem to enjoy playing together!**

あの子たち、気が合うみたいですね！

Ano kotachi, ki ga au mitai desu ne!

④ **Hey you two, don't fight, okay?**

ほら、けんかしちゃだめだよ！

Hora, kenka shicha dame da yo!

⑤ **Do you come here regularly?**

ここへは、よく来られるんですか？

Koko e wa, yoku korareru n' desu ka?

⑥ **Looks like someone's getting tired.**

あれ～？　ちょっと疲れちゃったかな～？

Arē? Chotto tsukarechatta ka nā?

⑦ **Want to set up a play date at my house?**

こんど、うちで子供たちを遊ばせない？

Kondo, uchi de kodomotachi o asobasenai?

# Nursery School

MP3
16_04

① **Is there a good nursery school in our area?**

この近所に、いい保育園はありますか？

Kono kinjo ni, ii hoikuen wa arimasu ka?

**②** **I'd be happier with an international nursery.**

インターナショナルの保育園があれば、

いちばんいいんだけど。

Intānashonaru no hoikuen ga areba,
ichiban ii n' da kedo.

**③** **May I see your facilities and classes?**

施設や保育現場を見学させてもらえますか？

Shisetsu ya hoiku-gemba o kengaku sasete moraemasu ka?

**④** **When is the deadline for application?**

願書の締め切りは、いつですか？

Gansho no shimekiri wa, itsu desu ka?

**⑤** **Can I enroll my child for half-days only?**

午前保育だけ、というのは可能ですか？

Gozen-hoiku dake, to iu no wa kanō desu ka?

**⑥** **What are the fees?**

保育料はおいくらですか？

Hoikuryō wa o-ikura desu ka?

**⑦** **She cried her first few days, but she's okay now.**

最初の２、３日は泣いたけど、いまはもう、

だいじょうぶになりました。

Saisho no ni, sannichi wa naita kedo, ima wa mō,
daijōbu ni narimashita.

⑧ **Do you have rules and guidelines in English?**

こちらの規則や方針を英語で書いたものは

ありますか？

Kochira no kisoku ya hōshin o Eigo de kaita mono wa
arimasu ka?

---

# Kindergarten

MP3
16_05

---

① **I'm torn between a public and private school.**

公立にしようか、私立にしようか、迷っています。

Kōritsu ni shiyō ka, shiritsu ni shiyō ka, mayotte imasu.

---

② **The uniforms and school supplies are costly.**

制服とか、持ち物とか、いろいろお金がかかるよね。

Seifuku to ka, mochimono to ka, iroiro o-kane ga kakaru yo ne.

---

③ **My boy seems to be fighting at school a lot.**

F うちの子、幼稚園でしょっちゅう

ケンカしてるらしいの。

Uchi no ko, yōchien de shotchū
kenka shite 'ru rashii no.

---

④ **Is my child learning Japanese characters?**

うちの子、日本語の読み書き、教わっていますか？

Uchi no ko, Nihongo no yomikaki, osowatte imasu ka?

⑤ **Am I expected to be involved in this event?**

この行事は、親も参加するんですか？

Kono gyōji wa, oya mo sanka suru n' desu ka?

⑥ **I feel buried under all these instructions!**

配られるプリントが多すぎて、わけがわかりません！

Kubarareru purinto ga ōsugite, wake ga wakarimasen!

⑦ **Is there a mom here who can help me read this?**

わたしに読めない字を教えてくれるおかあさん、

だれか、いませんか？

Watashi ni yomenai ji o oshiete kureru okā-san,
dareka imasen ka?

⑧ **My daughter speaks Japanese better than I do.**

うちの娘は、わたしより上手に
日本語を話します。

Uchi no musume wa, watashi yori jōzu ni
Nihongo o hanashimasu.

⑨ **What do we need to prepare for the outing?**

遠足には、どんなものを準備すればいいですか？

Ensoku ni wa, donna mono o jumbi sureba ii desu ka?

⑩ **How can I help out at school this year?**

今年は、どんな行事のお手伝いがありますか？

Kotoshi wa, donna gyōji no o-tetsudai ga arimasu ka?

# Elementary School

① **How long should daily homework take?**

毎日の宿題は、何時間くらいやらせれば

いいんでしょうか？

Mainichi no shukudai wa, nanjikan kurai yarasereba
ii n' deshō ka?

② **My son's in Mr. Tanaka's homeroom class.**

うちの息子は、田中先生のクラスです。

Uchi no musuko wa, Tanaka-sensei no kurasu desu.

③ **Will my daughter be able to assimilate here easily?**

うちの子、この学校でうまく

やっていけるでしょうか？

Uchi no ko, kono gakkō de umaku
yatte ikeru deshō ka?

④ **What after-school activities are available?**

放課後の活動には、どんなものがありますか？

Hōkago no katsudō ni wa, donna mono ga arimasu ka?

⑤ **Is my son doing well in your class?**

うちの子、学校で、ちゃんとやっていますか？

Uchi no ko, gakkō de, chanto yatte imasu ka?

⑥ **I'm concerned that my daughter is being bullied.**

うちの子、いじめにあってるんじゃないか、
心配なんですが……。

Uchi no ko, ijime ni atte 'ru n' ja nai ka,
shimpai nan desu ga . . .

⑦ **Can we meet to talk about David's progress?**

デイヴィッドの勉強のことで、
面談をお願いできますか？

Deibiddo no benkyō no koto de,
mendan o onegai dekimasu ka?

⑧ **I need to excuse my son from class today.**

きょうは子供を休ませますので、
よろしくお願いします。

Kyō wa kodomo o yasumasemasu no de,
yoroshiku onegai shimasu.

# Middle School and High School

MP3
16_07

① **Do most kids here also attend cram school?**

ここの生徒たちは、みんな塾に通ってるんですか？

Koko no seitotachi wa, minna juku ni kayotte 'ru n' desu ka?

② **I'd like to get more details on the student body.**

在校生の家庭環境などについて、
もう少し知りたいのですが。

Zaikōsei no katei-kankyō nado ni tsuite,
mō sukoshi shiritai no desu ga.

③ **Are there any other foreigners who attend?**

ほかにも外国人の生徒はいますか？

Hoka ni mo gaikokoujin no seito wa imasu ka?

④ **Can my son get tutoring in language arts?**

うちの子に国語の補習をお願いできますか？

Uchi no ko ni kokugo no hoshū o onegai dekimasu ka?

⑤ **I would very much like to join the PTA.**

ぜひPTAに参加したいと思います。

Zehi pī-tī-ē ni sanka shitai to omoimasu.

⑥ **Can you give me a rough idea of the annual costs?**

年間の学費は、だいたいどのくらいですか？

Nenkan no gakuhi wa, daitai dono kurai desu ka?

⑦ **Can you explain the grading system please?**

成績評価の基準を教えていただけますか？

Seiseki-hyōka no kijun o oshiete itadakemasu ka?

Babies, Kids, and Teens

# University

① **I'd like to study here for my year abroad.**

この大学に1年間留学したいと考えています。

Kono daigaku ni ichinenkan ryūgaku shitai to kangaete imasu.

② **I'm on an exchange program for a semester.**

交換留学制度で、1学期間だけこの大学に
来ています。

Kōkan-ryūgakuseido de, ichigakkikan dake kono daigaku
ni kite imasu.

③ **Can you tell me where the chem building is?**

化学科の教室はどこか、わかりますか？

Kagakuka no kyōshitsu wa doko ka, wakarimasu ka?

④ **The downtown campus is more convenient.**

都心にあるキャンパスのほうが便利ですね。

Toshin ni aru kyampasu no hō ga benri desu ne.

⑤ **I'm on a fellowship studying law.**

わたしは法学部のフェローシップ留学生です。

Watashi wa hōgakubu no ferōshippu ryūgakusei desu.

⑥ **I don't think they take college very seriously.**

大学生は、あまり勉強熱心じゃないみたいですね。

Daigakusei wa, amari benkyō-nesshin ja nai mitai desu ne.

## Alternative Education

MP3
16_09

① **Is there an affordable international school here?**

近くに、学費が手ごろな

インターナショナル・スクールはありますか？

Chikaku ni, gakuhi ga tegoro na
intānashonaru sukūru wa arimasu ka?

② **Are there local Steiner or Montessori schools?**

このあたりで、シュタイナーか
モンテッソーリの学校はありますか？

Kono atari de, Shutainā ka
Montessōri no gakkō wa arimasu ka?

③ **We're opting for homeschooling this year.**

今年はホーム・スクーリングにしようと
思っています。

Kotoshi wa hōmu sukūringu ni shiyō to
omotte imasu.

④ **Are there any bilingual playgroups around?**

このへんにバイリンガルの保育施設はありますか？

Kono hen ni bairingaru no hoiku-shisetsu wa arimasu ka?

**Babies, Kids, and Teens**

⑤ **Can you recommend a good math tutor who can speak English?**

英語が話せる数学の家庭教師、
だれか紹介してもらえませんか？

Eigo ga hanaseru sūgaku no kateikyōshi,
dareka shōkai shite moraemasen ka?

---

⑥ **I'm looking for a private piano teacher.**

ピアノの個人レッスンをしてくれる先生を
探しています。

Piano no kojin ressun o shite kureru sensei o
sagashite imasu.

---

⑦ **I need a teacher who can explain grammar.**

文法をわかりやすく教えてくれる先生、
いませんかね。

Bumpō o wakariyasuku oshiete kureru sensei,
imasen ka ne.

---

# Talking to Other People's Kids

16_10

① **You look like you're having fun.**

楽しそうだね。
Tanoshisō da ne.

② **What school are you from?**

どこの学校に行ってるの？

Doko no gakkō ni itteru no?

③ **Are you on a class outing?**

学校の遠足で来たの？

Gakkō no ensoku de kita no?

④ **How come you're not in school?**

きょうは、どうして学校に行かないの？

Kyō wa, dōshite gakkō ni ikanai no?

⑤ **Are you okay?**

だいじょうぶ？

Daijōbu?

⑥ **Are you lost?**

迷子になったの？

Maigo ni natta no?

⑦ **Wait and I'll go get help.**

ちょっと待って、いまだれか呼んでくるから。

Chotto matte, ima dareka yonde kuru kara.

⑧ **Are you allowed to do that?**

そんなことして、いいの？

Sonna koto shite ii no?

⑨ **Hey, stop!**

ちょっと、やめなさい！

Chotto, yamenasai!

Babies, Kids, and Teens

⑩　**You guys are a noisy bunch.**

F　あなたたち、騒<ruby>が<rt>さわ</rt></ruby>しいですよ。

Anatatachi, sawagashii desu yo.

M　きみたち、騒<ruby>が<rt>さわ</rt></ruby>しいぞ。

Kimitachi, sawagashii zo.

---

### A Kid's Life

With kids comes a whole sandbox of special words that might come in handy:

| | | |
|---|---|---|
| afternoon snack | **oyatsu** | おやつ |
| amusement park | **yūenchi** | 遊園地 |
| baby powder | **bebīpaudā** | ベビー・パウダー |
| baby food | **bebīfūdo** | ベビー・フード |
| baby formula | **konamiruku** | 粉ミルク |
| baby stroller | **bebīkā** | ベビーカー |
| beach | **umi/bīchi** | 海／ビーチ |
| box lunch | **o-bentō** | お弁当 |
| campground | **kyampujō** | キャンプ場 |
| diapers | **omutsu** | おむつ |
| festival | **o-matsuri** | お祭り |
| game center | **gēsen** | ゲーセン |
| junk food | **janku-fūdo** | ジャンク・フード |
| park | **kōen** | 公園 |
| playground | **undojō** | 運動場 |
| pool | **pūru** | プール |
| sandbox | **sunaba** | 砂場 |
| sweets | **okashi** | お菓子 |
| zoo | **dōbutsuen** | 動物園 |

## Calls for Help

**MP3**
17_01

① **Help!**
助けて〜！
Tasuketē!

② **I can't swim!**
おぼれる〜！
Oborerū!

③ **I'm feeling really queasy.**
胸がむかむかして、気もち悪いんです。
Mune ga mukamuka shite, kimochi warui n' desu.

④ **I think I'm going to be sick.**
吐きそう……。
Hakisō . . .

⑤ **I think I'm going to pass out.**
気が遠くなりそう……。
Ki ga tōku narisō . . .

⑥ **This is really serious.**
非常に深刻な状態です。
Hijō ni shinkoku na jōtai desu.

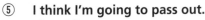

⑦ **I really need a doctor right now!**

すぐ、医者を呼んで！

Sugu, isha o yonde!

---

⑧ **I think we'd better call an ambulance.**

救急車を呼んだほうがいいと思う。

Kyūkyūsha o yonda hō ga ii to omou.

---

⑨ **Oh my god, get help quick!**

たいへん！　早く助けを呼んで！

Taihen! Hayaku tasuke o yonde!

---

⑩ **There's been a terrible accident.**

ひどい事故です。

Hidoi jiko desu.

---

# Ambulance

**MP3**

**17_02**

---

① **We need an ambulance immediately.**

救急車、すぐ来てください。

Kyūkyūsha, sugu kite kudasai.

---

② **My friend is bleeding and he's nearly unconscious.**

友だちが出血してて、

ほとんど意識がないんです。

Tomodachi ga shukketsu shite 'te,
hotondo ishiki ga nai n' desu.

③ **She just passed out all of a sudden.**

突然、気を失ったんです。

Totsuzen, ki o ushinatta n' desu.

④ **Should I perform CPR?**

心肺蘇生をやったほうがいいですか？

Shimpai-sosei o yatta hō ga ii desu ka?

⑤ **We need a paramedic!**

救急救命士は、いませんか!?

Kyūkyū-kyūmeishi wa imasen ka!?

⑥ **He has a fever and he's delirious.**

高熱で、意識が乱れています。

Kōnetsu de, ishiki ga midarete imasu.

⑦ **He's been badly burned.**

ひどいやけどです。

Hidoi yakedo desu.

⑧ **I don't know this person, but he's very sick.**

知らない人なんですけど、

すごくぐあいが悪そうなんです。

Shiranai hito nan desu kedo,

sugoku guai ga warusō nan desu.

⑨ **She fell and may have broken a bone.**

転んだんです。骨が折れてるかもしれません。

Koronda n' desu. Hone ga orete 'ru ka mo shiremasen.

# Hospital

MP3
17_03

① **We need a doctor now.**

すぐに診てください。

Sugu ni mite kudasai.

---

② **Where's the emergency room?**

救急は、どっちですか？

Kyūkyū wa, dotchi desu ka?

---

③ **She was fine this morning, but then lost consciousness.**

けさは普通だったんですけど、

そのあと意識がなくなったんです。

Kesa wa futsū datta n' desu kedo,

sono ato ishiki ga nakunatta n' desu.

---

④ **Can I go with him, please?**

付き添って行って、いいですか？

Tsukisotte itte, ii desu ka?

---

⑤ **Can you tell me if it's serious?**

深刻な状態でしょうか？

Shinkoku na jōtai deshō ka?

---

⑥ **Where should I wait?**

どこで待てば、いいですか？

Doko de mateba, ii desu ka?

⑦ **Here's my medical insurance card.**

保険証、ここにあります。

Hokenshō, koko ni arimasu.

---

# Fire and Police

① **I need to report a fire.**

火事です！

Kaji desu!

---

② **There's a lot of smoke coming from next door.**

となりの家から煙がたくさん出ています。

Tonari no ie kara kemuri ga takusan dete imasu.

---

③ **Please hurry, I think there are people still inside.**

早く！　まだ、中に人がいます！

Hayaku! Mada, naka ni hito ga imasu!

---

④ **There was an explosion, and then flames.**

爆発があって、そのあと火が出ました。

Bakuhatsu ga atte, sono ato hi ga demashita.

---

⑤ **It's a false alarm—I just burnt some toast.**

いまのは、まちがって鳴ったんです。

トーストを焦がしただけです。

Ima no wa, machigatte natta n' desu.

Tōsuto o kogashita dake desu.

⑥ **I need to report a burglary.**

ドロボウにはいられました。

Dorobō ni hairaremashita.

---

⑦ **My watch, jewelry, and cash are missing.**

時計と宝石類と現金がなくなっています。

Tokei to hōsekirui to genkin ga naku natte imasu.

---

⑧ **There's a robbery happening across the street.**

通りの向かいで、強盗事件が発生しました。

Tōri no mukai de, gōtō-jiken ga hassei shimashita.

---

⑨ **Two guys are fighting in the restaurant.**

レストランで、男二人がけんかしています。

Resutoran de, otoko futari ga kenka shite imasu.

---

⑩ **Some drunks are creating a disturbance.**

酔っぱらいが騒いでいます。

Yopparai ga sawaide imasu.

---

# Traffic Accidents and Incidents

MP3

17_05

① **She ran a red light and hit me broadside.**

むこうが赤信号を無視して、
横から突っ込んできたんです。

Mukō ga akashingō o mushi shite,
yoko kara tsukkonde kita n' desu.

② **It was the other driver's fault.**
悪<sup>わる</sup>いのは、むこうです。
Warui no wa, mukō desu.

③ **I couldn't brake in time, and rear-ended him.**
ブレーキが遅<sup>おく</sup>れて、追突<sup>ついとつ</sup>してしまいました。
Burēki ga okurete, tsuitotsu shite shimaimashita.

④ **He was definitely speeding.**
明<sup>あき</sup>らかにスピードの出<sup>だ</sup>しすぎだと思<sup>おも</sup>います。
Akiraka ni supīdo no dashisugi da to omoimasu.

⑤ **I was going well below the speed limit.**
わたしは、制限速度<sup>せいげんそくど</sup>よりずっと遅<sup>おそ</sup>いスピード

でした。
Watashi wa, seigensokudo yori zutto osoi supīdo
deshita.

⑥ **What's the problem, Officer?**
はい、何<sup>なん</sup>でしょうか？
Hai, nan deshō ka?

⑦ **I didn't realize this was a one-way street.**
一方通行<sup>いっぽうつうこう</sup>だとは気<sup>き</sup>が付<sup>つ</sup>きませんでした。
Ippōtsūkō da to wa ki ga tsukimasen deshita.

⑧ **Am I going to lose my license?**
免許取<sup>めんきょと</sup>り消<sup>け</sup>しになりますか？
Menkyo torikeshi ni narimasu ka?

⑨ **Please don't give me a parking ticket—
I'll move it right away.**

お願い、キップ切らないで！

いますぐ移動しますから。

Onegai, kippu kiranaide!

Ima sugu idō shimasu kara.

## Fight and Flight

MP3
17_06

① **We had an argument and he punched me.**

言い合いになって、彼がわたしを殴ったんです。

Iiai ni natte, kare ga watashi o nagutta n' desu.

② **I have no idea why she attacked me.**

どうして彼女が襲いかかってきたのか、

見当もつきません。

Dōshite kanojo ga osoikakatte kita no ka,

kentō mo tsukimasen.

③ **He had a knife and threatened me.**

あの男にナイフで脅されました。

Ano otoko ni naifu de odosaremashita.

④ **I got scared and I ran away.**

怖くなって、走って逃げました。

Kowaku natte, hashitte nigemashita.

⑤ **That man pushed her onto the tracks.**

あの男が、女の人を線路に突き落としたんです。

Ano otoko ga, onna-no-hito o senro ni tsukiotoshita n' desu.

⑥ **I was walking home and my bag was snatched.**

家に歩いて帰るとちゅうで、

バッグをひったくられました。

Ie ni aruite kaeru tochū de,
baggu o hittakuraremashita.

⑦ **The demonstration got out of hand and I left.**

デモがだんだん荒れてきたので、

その場を離れました。

Demo ga dandan arete kita no de,
sono ba o hanaremashita.

⑧ **I'm just an innocent bystander!**

わたしは、たまたま目撃しただけです。

Watashi wa, tamatama mokugeki shita dake desu.

⑨ **I was only trying to stop the fight.**

わたしは、ただ、けんかを止めようと

しただけです。

Watashi wa, tada, kenka o tomeyō to
shita dake desu.

## Dangers

MP3

17_07

---

① **What time is the typhoon supposed to hit?**

台風、何時ごろ上陸するって？

Taifū, nanji-goro jōriku suru tte?

---

② **How big was the earthquake?**

震度は？

Shindo wa?

---

③ **Where's the nearest evacuation site?**

ここからいちばん近い避難場所は、どこですか？

Koko kara ichiban chikai hinan-basho wa, doko desu ka?

---

④ **What should I put in my earthquake kit?**

非常持出袋は、何を入れておけばいいかな？

Hijō-mochidashibukuro wa, nani o irete okeba ii ka na?

---

⑤ **Is there any danger of a tidal wave?**

津波、来そうなの？

Tsunami, kisō na no?

---

⑥ **They said there was a good chance of flooding.**

洪水になるかもしれないんだって。

Kōzui ni naru ka mo shirenai n' datte.

---

⑦ **I really hate electrical storms.**

かみなり、だいっきらい。

Kaminari, daikkirai.

⑧ **We need to conserve water because of the drought.**

日照りが続いてるから、節水しなくちゃね。

Hideri ga tsuzuite 'ru kara, sessui shinakucha ne.

⑨ **What exactly is photochemical smog?**

光化学スモッグって、どういうものなの？

Kōkagaku-sumoggu tte, dō iu mono na no?

# Train Situations

MP3

17_08

① **Excuse me, I'm not your pillow.**

すみません、わたし、
あなたの枕じゃないんですけど。

Sumimasen, watashi,
anata no makura ja nai n' desu kedo.

② **Pervert!**

痴漢！

Chikan!

③ **Why are we stopping here?**

電車、どうして止まったんですか？

Densha, dōshite tomatta n' desu ka?

④ **I lost my ticket.**

切符をなくしてしまいました。

Kippu o nakushite shimaimashita.

⑤ **He was molesting me.**

あの男<ruby>男<rt>おとこ</rt></ruby>に<ruby>痴漢<rt>ちかん</rt></ruby>されました。

Ano otoko ni chikan saremashita.

⑥ **Hey, watch it!**

F ちょっと、<ruby>気<rt>き</rt></ruby>を<ruby>付<rt>つ</rt></ruby>けてよ！

Chotto, ki o tsukete yo!

M おい、<ruby>気<rt>き</rt></ruby>を<ruby>付<rt>つ</rt></ruby>けろよ！

Oi, ki o tsukero yo!

⑦ **I hate being packed like sardines.**

こんなぎゅうぎゅう<ruby>詰<rt>づ</rt></ruby>め、かんべんしてほしいよ。

Konna gyūgyū-zume, kamben shite hoshii yo.

⑧ **Excuse me, could you slide over please?**

すみません、<ruby>少<rt>すこ</rt></ruby>し<ruby>詰<rt>つ</rt></ruby>めていただけますか？

Sumimasen, sukoshi tsumete itadakemasu ka?

⑨ **Push the emergency button!**

<ruby>非常<rt>ひじょう</rt></ruby>ボタン<ruby>押<rt>お</rt></ruby>して！

Hijō-botan oshite!

# Panic at the Disco

MP3
17_09

① **Buzz off!**

F さっさと<ruby>消<rt>き</rt></ruby>えてよ！

Sassa to kiete yo!

② **Look, I'm with someone, okay?**

だから、連れがいるんだ、って！

Da kara, tsure ga irunda tte!

③ **I came here to just chill by myself, thanks.**

F 悪いわね、ちょっと休んでるだけなの。

Warui wa ne, chotto yasunde 'ru dake na no.

M 悪い、ちょっと休んでるだけなんだ。

Warui, chotto yasunde 'ru dake nan da.

④ **Maybe another time.**

また、いつか。

Mata, itsuka.

⑤ **Forget it, okay?**

興味、ないから。

Kyōmi, nai kara.

⑥ **That guy over there is really bothering me.**

あそこにいる男、ほんと、うっとうしいんだけど。

Asoko ni iru otoko, honto, uttōshii n' da kedo.

⑦ **That girl is stalking me, and I think she's drunk.**

あの女、しつこいんだよ。

酔っぱらってんじゃないか？

Ano onna, shitsukoi n' da yo.

Yopparatte n' ja nai ka?

⑧ **Cool it or we'll both end up in trouble.**

M そのくらいにしとけ。めんどうなことになるぞ。

Sono kurai ni shitoke. Mendō na koto ni naru zo.

F そのくらいにしとけば？

めんどうなことになるわよ。

Sono kurai ni shitokeba?

Mendō na koto ni naru wa yo.

⑨ **Leave me alone or I'll call the cops.**

F ほっといてくれない？ 警察呼ぶわよ。

Hottoite kurenai? Keisatsu yobu wa yo.

---

### Getting Help

Tip One: It's crucial to know the location of the nearest **koban,** or "police box," a mini–police station situated in nearly every neighborhood. Many complaints and calls for help can be answered by the **koban.**

Tip Two: The emergency number for fire and ambulance in Japan is 119. For police, 110.

Tip Three: If you need to get somewhere in a hurry, hop in a cab and say, (place name) **made onegai shimasu.**

| emergency room | **kyūmei-kyūkyū sentā** | 救命救急センター |
| emergency shelter | **hinanjo** | 避難所 |
| hospital | **byōin** | 病院 |
| U.S. Embassy | **Amerika Taishikan** | アメリカ大使館 |

## Births, Birthdays, and Anniversaries

**18_01**

① **It's a girl!**

女の子です！

Onna-no-ko desu!

② **She was born at five A.M. and weighs 3,456 grams.**

朝の5時に生まれました。

体重は3456グラムです。

Asa no goji ni umaremashita.

Taijū wa sanzen-yonhyaku-gojūroku guramu desu.

③ **Please welcome our new baby boy, Jason.**

はじめまして、わが家のニュー・フェイス、

ジェイソンです。

Hajimemashite, wagaya no nyūfeisu,

Jeison desu.

④ **Congratulations on your beautiful baby!**

おめでとう、かわいい赤ちゃんだね！

Omedetō, kawaii akachan da ne!

⑤ **Happy birthday!**
お誕生日、おめでとう！
O-tanjōbi, omedetō!

⑥ **Happy 30th anniversary.**
結婚30周年、おめでとう。
Kekkon sanjusshūnen, omedetō.

⑦ **It's our golden anniversary.**
わたしたち、今年、金婚式なんです。
Watashitachi, kotoshi, kinkonshiki nan desu.

⑧ **Please help us celebrate John's 18th birthday.**
ジョンの18歳の誕生祝いをするので、ぜひ、
いらしてください。
Jon no jūhassai no tanjō-iwai o suru no de, zehi,
irashite kudasai.

⑨ **It's not every day you turn 60.**
60歳のお誕生日は、特別ですよ。
Rokujussai no o-tanjōbi wa, tokubetsu desu yo.

# Engagements and Weddings

**18_02**

① **Will you marry me?**
結婚してくれますか？
Kekkonshite kuremasu ka?

② **I'd like to tell everyone, we're engaged!**

F みなさ〜ん、わたしたち婚約しました！

Minasān, watashitachi kon'yaku shimashita!

M みなさ〜ん、ぼくたち婚約しました！

Minasān, bokutachi kon'yaku shimashita!

③ **We're planning to get married this spring.**

わたしたち、この春に結婚する予定です。

Watashitachi, kono haru ni kekkon suru yotei desu.

④ **We've already registered at the ward office.**

もう、区役所に婚姻届を出してきました。

Mō, kuyakusho ni kon'in-todoke o dashite kimashita.

⑤ **Will you come to my wedding?**

結婚式に出席してくれますか？

Kekkonshiki ni shusseki shite kuremasu ka?

⑥ **Please join us at the reception party.**

披露宴にお招きしたいのですが。

Hirōen ni omaneki shitai no desu ga.

⑦ **I can't believe you're getting married!**

M おまえが結婚するなんて、信じられないよ！

Omae ga kekkon suru nante, shinjirarenai yo!

F あなたが結婚するなんて、信じられないわよ！

Anata ga kekkon suru nante, shinjirarenai wa yo!

⑧ **You are the luckiest couple alive.**

最高にお似合いのカップルだね！

Saikō ni oniai no kappuru da ne!

## School Events

MP3

18_03

① **My daughter is just starting high school.**

うちの娘は、高校にはいったばかりです。

Uchi no musume wa, kōkō ni haitta bakari desu.

② **She got into Harvard on a scholarship.**

彼女は、奨学金をもらってハーバードに
行きました。

Kanojo wa, shōgakukin o moratte Hābādo ni
ikimashita.

③ **My grades this semester were great.**

今学期の成績は、すごく良かったよ。

Kongakki no seiseki wa, sugoku yokatta yo.

④ **He has to transfer schools next year.**

あの子、来年転校しちゃうんだ。

Ano ko, rainen tenkō shichau n' da.

⑤ **We're applying to a boarding school.**

全寮制の学校に願書を出しています。

Zenryōsei no gakkō ni gansho o dashite imasu.

⑥ **She seems to be adjusting to school well.**

あの子は学校でうまくやっているようです。

Ano ko wa gakkō de umaku yatte iru yō desu.

⑦ **She's going to the school dance with a date.**

彼女、ボーイフレンドと学校の

ダンス・パーティーに行くらしいよ。

Kanojo, bōifurendo to gakkō no

dansu pātī ni iku rashii yo.

⑧ **He's got a lead role in the school play.**

あの子、学芸会で主役をもらったんだよ。

Ano ko, gakugeikai de shuyaku o moratta n' da yo.

## Company Events

MP3
18_04

① **We're celebrating our company's 10th anniversary.**

わが社は、今年、創業10周年を迎えます。

Wagasha wa, kotoshi sōgyō jusshūnen o mukaemasu.

② **We're holding a retirement party for John on the 16th.**

こんどの16日に、

ジョンの退職記念パーティーを開きます。

Kondo no jūrokunichi ni,

Jon no taishoku kinen pātī o hirakimasu.

---

③ **There's been a change in personnel.**

人事異動があったんだ。

Jinji-idō ga atta n' da.

---

④ **I'll be leaving to head up our Singapore office.**

このたび、シンガポール支社長を拝命し、
現地へ赴くこととなりました。

Kono tabi, Shingapōru shishachō o haimei shi,
genchi e omomuku koto to narimashita.

---

⑤ **I'll never forget the years I've worked here.**

ここでみなさんとがんばった日々のことは、
忘れません。

Koko de minasan to gambatta hibi no koto wa,
wasuremasen.

---

## Personal Events and Milestones

MP3
18_05

---

① **I'm giving a piano concert, if you want to come.**

こんど、ピアノの発表会があるんだけど、
来てもらえたら、うれしいな……。

Kondo, piano no happyōkai ga aru n' da kedo,
kite moraetara, ureshii na . . .

② **I'm going to my 25th high school reunion next week.**

来週、高校の卒業25周年の同窓会に
行くんだ。

Raishū, kōkō no sotsugyō nijūgoshūnen no dōsōkai ni iku n' da.

③ **It's really hard being an empty nester.**

F 子育てが終わって、空の巣症候群……つらいわ。

Kosodate ga owatte, kara-no-su-shōkōgun . . . tsurai wa.

④ **I've decided it's time to change careers.**

いまが転職のチャンスだと思ってね。

Ima ga tenshoku no chansu da to omotte ne.

⑤ **She's just really in need of a life change.**

彼女、こうなったら生き方を変えたほうがいいね。

Kanojo, kō nattara ikikata o kaeta hō ga ii ne.

⑥ **I may be 60, but I don't feel a day over 30.**

年は60でも、気もちは30だよ。

Toshi wa rokujū demo, kimochi wa sanjū da yo.

⑦ **She's in menopause.**

彼女は、いま更年期なんです。

Kanojo wa, ima kōnenki nan desu.

⑧ **I've decided that I'm never going to drink again.**

アルコールは、きっぱりとやめることにしたよ。

Arukōru wa, kippari to yameru koto ni shita yo.

⑨ **I think it's time for me to move on.**

そろそろ先へ進む時期だと思ってね。

Sorosoro saki e susumu jiki da to omotte ne.

⑩ **I'm falling in love for the first time in my life.**

M 生まれて初めて、恋してるんだ……。

Umarete hajimete, koishite 'ru n' da ...

F 生まれて初めて、恋してるの……。

Umarete hajimete, koishite 'ru no ...

## Holiday Events

18_06

① **Happy New Year!**

あけまして、おめでとうございます！

Akemashite omedetō gozaimasu!

② **I hear we get a day off on the vernal equinox.**

春分の日って、休みなんだってね。

Shumbun no hi tte, yasumi nan da tte ne.

③ **Next month we celebrate Passover.**

来月は「過ぎ越しの祭り」です。

Raigetsu wa "Sugikoshi no Matsuri" desu.

④ **Tomorrow's a bank holiday back home.**

わたしの国では、明日は祝日です。

Watashi no kuni de wa, asu wa shukujitsu desu.

⑤ **Monday is a national holiday.**

こんどの月曜日<small>げつようび</small>は、祝日<small>しゅくじつ</small>ですよ。

Kondo no Getsuyōbi wa, shukujitsu desu yo.

⑥ **I just love three-day weekends.**

週末<small>しゅうまつ</small>の三連休<small>さんれんきゅう</small>って、ほんと、うれしいよね。

Shūmatsu no sanrenkyū tte, honto, ureshii yo ne.

⑦ **Christmas is coming.**

もうすぐ、クリスマスだね。

Mō sugu, Kurisumasu da ne.

⑧ **Which foreign holidays are popular here?**

外国<small>がいこく</small>の祝日<small>しゅくじつ</small>で、日本<small>にほん</small>でも
よく知<small>し</small>られているのは何<small>なん</small>の日<small>ひ</small>ですか?

Gaikoku no shukujitsu de, Nihon demo
yoku shirarete iru no wa nan no hi desu ka?

⑨ **We plan to party all night on New Year's Eve.**

大<small>おお</small>みそかは、朝<small>あさ</small>までパーティーの予定<small>よてい</small>です。

Ōmisoka wa, asa made pātī no yotei desu.

## Funerals

MP3
18_07

① **Did you hear about Ueda-san's passing?**

上田<small>うえだ</small>さんが亡<small>な</small>くなったって、聞<small>き</small>いた?

Ueda-san ga nakunatta tte, kiita?

② **I'm sorry to tell you my father has just died.**

父が、少し前に亡くなりました。

Chichi ga, sukoshi mae ni nakunarimashita.

③ **This is so sudden.**

本当に、突然のことでしたね。

Hontō ni, totsuzen no koto deshita ne.

④ **I am very sorry to hear the news.**

まことに、ご愁傷様です。

Makoto ni, goshūshōsama desu.

⑤ **This must be very hard for your family.**

ご家族のみなさまは、さぞ、おつらいでしょうね。

Go-kazoku no minasama wa, sazo, otsurai deshō ne.

⑥ **If there is anything I can do, please call me.**

わたしにできることがあれば、
何でもおっしゃってください。

Watashi ni dekiru koto ga areba,
nandemo osshatte kudasai.

⑦ **Her passing brings us all great sorrow.**

彼女が亡くなって、わたしたち、みんな、
とても悲しいです。

Kanojo ga nakunatte, watashitachi minna,
totemo kanashii desu.

⑧ **Please accept my sincere condolences.**

心からお悔やみ申し上げます。

Kokoro kara okuyami mōshiagemasu.

⑨ **I want to send flowers with our condolences.**

お悔やみのしるしに、
お花をお届けしたいのですが。

Okuyami no shirushi ni,
o-hana o otodoke shitai no desu ga.

## Stressful Challenges

18_08

① **Regretfully, she and I are going to divorce.**

残念だけど、ぼくたち、離婚することになったんだ。

Zannen da kedo, bokutachi, rikon suru kotoni natta n' da.

② **They're fighting over child custody.**

あの二人、子供の親権で、もめてるんだよ。

Ano futari, kodomo no shinken de, momete 'ru n' da yo.

③ **I was hospitalized after the accident.**

事故にあって、入院していました。

Jiko ni atte, nyūin shite imashita.

④ **I lost my wallet and everything in it.**

財布をまるごと落としてしまいました。

Saifu o marugoto otoshite shimaimashita.

⑤ **She's been caring for her sick father.**

彼女、ずっと病気のお父さんの
看病をしていたんです。

Kanojo, zutto byōki no otō-san no
kambyō o shite ita n' desu.

⑥ **Her husband has Alzheimer's.**

彼女のご主人、アルツハイマー病なんです。

Kanojo no go-shujin, Arutsuhaimā-byō nan desu.

⑦ **He turned out to be physically abusive.**

F 彼、暴力をふるう人だ、ってわかったの。

Kare, bōryoku o furuu hito da tte wakatta no.

⑧ **She was just fired from her job.**

彼女、仕事をクビになったばかりなんだ。

Kanojo, shigoto o kubi ni natta bakari nan da.

⑨ **They may be facing bankruptcy.**

あの人たち、そのうち左前になるかもね。

Ano hitotachi, sono uchi hidarimae ni naru kamo ne.

# Achievements

MP3
18_09

① **I just completed my first marathon.**

ついこのあいだ、初めてマラソンを完走したんだ。

Tsui kono aida, hajimete marason o kansō shita n' da.

② **I got into Brown!**
ブラウン大学に受かったんだよ！
Buraun Daigaku ni ukatta n' da yo!

③ **I was just promoted.**
こんど、昇進したんだ。
Kondo, shōshin shita n' da.

④ **We finally paid off our loan.**
やっと、借金の返済が終わったよ。
Yatto, shakkin no hensai ga owatta yo.

⑤ **Our team made the playoffs.**
うちのチーム、プレーオフに進出したんだよ。
Uchi no chīmu, purēofu ni shinshutsu shita n' da yo.

⑥ **My picture was in the paper.**
F わたし、新聞に写真が出たの。
Watashi, shimbun ni shashin ga deta no.

M ぼく、新聞に写真が出たんだ。
Boku, shimbun ni shashin ga deta n' da.

⑦ **I was voted employee of the month.**
月間最優秀社員に選ばれたんだ。
Gekkan saiyūshū shain ni erabareta n' da.

⑧ **I've been awarded a research scholarship.**
奨学金がもらえることになったんです。
Shōgakukin ga moraeru koto ni natta n' desu.

Special Events

## Cultural Explorations

① **Can you teach me how to make sushi?**
お寿司のにぎり方、教えてくれる？
O-sushi no nigirikata, oshiete kureru?

② **I want to learn aikido.**
合気道を習いたいな。
Aikidō o naraitai na.

③ **I want to learn how to play the shamisen.**
三味線を習いたいです。
Shamisen o naraitai desu.

④ **Where can I learn to draw manga?**
まんがの描き方って、
どこへ行けば教えてもらえるかな？
Manga no kakikata tte,
doko e ikeba oshiete moraeru ka na?

⑤ **Is it expensive to study the tea ceremony?**
茶道のおけいこは、お金がかかりますか？
Sadō no o-keiko wa, o-kane ga kakarimasu ka?

⑥ **I want to join a taiko group.**

太鼓の同好会にはいりたいな。

Taiko no dōkōkai ni hairitai na.

⑦ **I'd like to do a language exchange.**

たがいに言葉を教えあうランゲージ・

エクスチェンジをやってみたいです。

Tagai ni kotoba o oshieau rangēji-
ekusuchenji o yatte mitai desu.

# Pets

**MP3**
**19_02**

① **Is there a good veterinarian nearby?**

この近くで、いい獣医さんを知りませんか？

Kono chikaku de, ii jūi-san o shirimasen ka?

② **Can I take my dog off leash here?**

ここは、犬のリードをはずしてもいいんですか？

Koko wa, inu no rīdo o hazushite mo ii n' desu ka?

③ **Can you watch my cat while I'm away?**

留守のあいだ、猫の世話をお願いしても

いいですか？

Rusu no aida, neko no sewa o onegai shite mo
ii desu ka?

④ **Please be careful, my dog jumps on people.**

気を付けて。うちの犬は人にとびつくから。

Ki o tsukete. Uchi no inu wa hito ni tobitsuku kara.

⑤ **Where did you get such a cute puppy?**

かわいい子犬だね。どこで手に入れたの？

Kawaii koinu da ne. Doko de te ni ireta no?

⑥ **Am I allowed to bring my dog in here?**

ここは、犬を連れて、はいれますか？

Koko wa, inu o tsurete hairemasu ka?

⑦ **We won these goldfish at a festival last year.**

この金魚、去年のお祭りですくってきたの。

Kono kingyo, kyonen no omatsuri de sukutte kita no.

# Sports

19_03

① **Want to play a quick game of tennis?**

軽くテニスなんか、どう？

Karuku tenisu nanka, dō?

② **I'm training for the Honolulu Marathon.**

ホノルル・マラソンめざして

トレーニングしています。

Honoruru Marason mezashite
torēningu shite imasu.

③ **I swim nearly every day.**

わたし、ほぼ毎日、泳いでいます。

Watashi, hobo mainichi, oyoide imasu.

④ **I'm taking golf lessons on Saturdays.**

毎週土曜日にゴルフ・レッスンに通っています。

Maishū Doyōbi ni gorufu-ressun ni kayotte imasu.

⑤ **Let's work out together at the gym sometime.**

こんど、一緒にジム行かない？

Kondo, issho ni jimu ikanai?

⑥ **I'm looking for an evening yoga class.**

夕方のヨガ・レッスンを探してるんだ。

Yūgata no yoga ressun o sagashite 'ru n' da.

⑦ **I like outdoor sports.**

わたしは、アウトドア・スポーツが好きです。

Watashi wa, autodoa-supōtsu ga suki desu.

⑧ **What baseball team do you root for?**

プロ野球、どこのファン？

Puroyakyū, doko no fan?

Just for Fun

# Rural Adventure

MP3
19_04

① **I want to climb Mt. Fuji before I leave Japan.**

日本にいるうちに、富士山に登っておきたいな。

Nihon ni iru uchi ni, Fujisan ni nobotte okitai na.

② **Where can I go to get away from it all?**

どこへ行けば、このわずらわしい日常から
逃れられるんだろう？

Doko e ikeba, kono wazurawashii nichijō kara
nogarerareru n' darō?

③ **Is there a campsite in the area?**

そのあたりにキャンプ場はありますか？

Sono atari ni kyampujō wa arimasu ka?

④ **I've heard hiking up Mt. Takao is easy.**

高尾山は楽に登れる、って聞いたよ。

Takaosan wa raku ni noboreru tte kiita yo.

⑤ **I'm hoping to see what Japan used to look like.**

昔の日本がどんなふうだったか、
見てみたいです。

Mukashi no Nihon ga donna fū datta ka,
mite mitai desu.

⑥ **What's the specialty of this area?**

このあたりの名物というと、何ですか？

Kono atari no meibutsu to iu to, nan desu ka?

⑦ **We want to find some outdoor hot springs.**

露天風呂のある温泉に行きたいです。

Rotemburo no aru onsen ni ikitai desu.

⑧ **We're looking for a place to pick apples.**

りんご狩<sup>が</sup>りができるところ、どっか知<sup>し</sup>らない？

Ringogari ga dekiru tokoro, dokka shiranai?

⑨ **I've never been there, but let's go explore.**

行<sup>い</sup>ったことないけど、おもしろそうだから
行<sup>い</sup>ってみようよ。

Itta koto nai kedo, omoshirosō da kara
itte miyō yo.

# Cooking

MP3

19_05

① **How about I cook you dinner tonight?**

M 今夜<sup>こんや</sup>は、ぼくがごはん作<sup>つく</sup>ろうか？

Kon'ya wa, boku ga gohan tsukurō ka?

F 今夜<sup>こんや</sup>は、わたしがごはん作<sup>つく</sup>ろうか？

Kon'ya wa, watashi ga gohan tsukurō ka?

② **Can you show me how to do that?**

どうやるの？　教<sup>おし</sup>えて。

Dō yaru no? Oshiete.

③ **I love to cook.**

料理<sup>りょうり</sup>は、大好<sup>だいす</sup>きです。

Ryōri wa, daisuki desu.

④ **I don't measure, I just go by taste.**

てきとうに目分量で、
あとは味見しながら作るんです。

Tekitō ni mebunryō de,
ato wa ajimi shinagara tsukuru n' desu.

⑤ **This is a complicated recipe.**

これ、手の込んだレシピなんだよ。

Kore, te no konda reshipi nanda yo.

⑥ **I need a much bigger pot.**

もっと大きい鍋がほしいな。

Motto ōkii nabe ga hoshii na.

⑦ **I'd like to learn a few traditional dishes.**

伝統料理の作り方を教わりたいです。

Dentō-ryōri no tsukurikata o osowaritai desu.

# Ryokans and Hot Springs

**MP3**

19_06

① **How old is this place?**

ここは、どのくらい昔からあるんですか？

Koko wa, dono kurai mukashi kara aru n' desu ka?

② **Is this food a local specialty?**

これは、この地方の名物料理ですか？

Kore wa, kono chihō no meibutsu-ryōri desu ka?

③ **Whoa, this towel is really small.**

わぁ、このタオル、小<sup>ちい</sup>さい！

Wā, kono taoru, chiisai!

④ **Why's the water that color?**

どうして、ここのお湯<sup>ゆ</sup>はこんな色<sup>いろ</sup>を
してるんですか？

Dōshite, koko no oyu wa konna iro o
shiteru n' desu ka?

⑤ **This makes my skin feel so soft.**

F わぁ、お肌<sup>はだ</sup>がすべすべになった！

Wā, o-hada ga subesube ni natta!

M おっ、肌<sup>はだ</sup>がすべすべになった！

O, hada ga subesube ni natta!

⑥ **I've never felt so relaxed in my life!**

こんなにのんびりしたのは、生<sup>う</sup>まれて初<sup>はじ</sup>めてです！

Konna ni nombiri shita no wa, umarete hajimete desu!

⑦ **This water is way too hot!**

このお湯<sup>ゆ</sup>、熱<sup>あっ</sup>すぎるよ！

Kono oyu, atsusugiru yo!

Just for Fun

# Museums and Galleries

**MP3**
19_07

① **Have you seen the Cézanne show yet?**

セザンヌ展、もう見た？

Sezannu-ten, mō mita?

---

② **Let's go gallery-hopping around Ginza.**

銀座で画廊めぐりしない？

Ginza de garō-meguri shinai?

---

③ **I prefer abstract work to realistic.**

写実画より抽象画のほうが好きだな。

Shajitsuga yori chūshōga no hō ga suki da na.

---

④ **I like both sculpture and paintings.**

彫刻も絵画も好きです。

Chōkoku mo kaiga mo suki desu.

---

⑤ **Does this museum have a pamphlet in English?**

この美術館には、英文のパンフレットが

ありますか？

Kono bijutsukan ni wa, Eibun no panfuretto ga
arimasu ka?

---

⑥ **What period is this work from?**

この作品は、何時代のものですか？

Kono sakuhin wa, nanijidai no mono desu ka?

⑦ **They have a collection of European oil paintings.**

あそこは、ヨーロッパの油絵コレクションを
所蔵しています。

Asoko wa, Yōroppa no aburae korekushon o
shozō shite imasu.

⑧ **Who did this installation?**

これは、だれの作品ですか？

Kore wa, dare no sakuhin desu ka?

# Sightseeing and Photography

MP3
19_08

① **I feel like such a tourist here!**

まるで、おのぼりさんみたいな
気分になっちゃうね！

Marude, onoborisan mitai na
kibun ni natchau ne!

② **I've always wanted to ride in one of these.**

こういうの、ずっと乗ってみたかったんだ。

Kō iu no, zutto notte mitakatta n' da.

③ **Can I take a snapshot of you two?**

お二人の写真、とらせてもらって、いいですか？

O-futari no shashin, torasete moratte ii desu ka?

Just for Fun

④ **I live here, but I never get a chance to sightsee.**

ここに住んでるのに、あらためて観光する

チャンスって、ないなぁ。

Koko ni sunde 'ru no ni, aratamete kankō suru
chansu tte, nai nā.

⑤ **Do you think it's okay if I take a picture of this?**

これ、写真とっても、かまわないと思う？

Kore, shashin totte mo kamawanai to omou?

⑥ **I need to get some stuff for my camera.**

ちょっと、カメラに必要なもの、買ってくるね。

Chotto, kamera ni hitsuyō na mono, katte kuru ne.

⑦ **Can I take a photo if I turn off the flash?**

フラッシュをたかなければ、写真撮影はOKですか？

Furasshu o takanakereba, shashin-satsuei wa ōkkē desu ka?

⑧ **What are the must-sees in Kyoto?**

京都観光で絶対はずせない場所って、

どこでしょうね？

Kyōto-kankō de zettai hazusenai basho tte,
doko deshō ne?

⑨ **I want a guided tour for the whole trip.**

全日程ガイド付きのツアーをお願いします。

Zennittei gaido-tsuki no tsuā o onegai shimasu.

# Concerts and Movies

① **Does the concert have reserved seating?**

そのコンサート、座席指定なの？

Sono konsāto, zaseki-shitei na no?

② **I've heard this band is absolutely awesome.**

このバンド、マジ、すごいらしいよ。

Kono bando, maji, sugoirashii yo.

③ **Let's set a meeting place in case we separate.**

はぐれたときに落ち合う場所、決めておこうよ。

Hagureta toki ni ochiau basho, kimete okō yo.

④ **Where can I get discount tickets?**

ディスカウント・チケットって、どこで買えるの？

Disukaunto chiketto tte, doko de kaeru no?

⑤ **I can't hear a thing you're saying!**

何言ってんのか、全然聞こえない！

Nani itte n' no ka, zenzen kikoenai!

⑥ **What time does the movie start?**

映画、何時から？

Eiga, nanji kara?

⑦ **Is it a comedy?**

それって、コメディ？

Sore tte, komedī?

⑧ **Is this movie too scary for little kids?**

この映画、小さい子には怖すぎるかな？

Kono eiga, chiisai ko ni wa kowasugiru ka na?

⑨ **Are there subtitles in English?**

英語の字幕は、あるの？

Eigo no jimaku wa, aru no?

⑩ **Let's rent some DVDs and hang out at my place.**

DVD借りて、うちでゆっくり見ようよ。

Dī-bui-dī karite, uchi de yukkuri miyō yo.

## Road Trips

MP3

19_10

① **Did you bring a map to this place?**

目的地までの地図、持ってきた？

Mokutekichi made no chizu, mottekita?

② **About how much will the tolls be?**

道路の通行料金、どのくらいかな？

Dōro no tsūkōryōkin, dono kurai ka na?

③ **We'll save a lot of money if we carpool.**

相乗りすれば、かなりお金を節約できるよ。

Ainori sureba, kanari o-kane o setsuyaku dekiru yo.

④ **Looks like we're running low on gas.**

ガス欠になりそう……。

Gasuketsu ni narisō . . .

⑤ **You'd better pull over and ask for directions.**

車を止めて、道を聞いたほうがいいよ。

Kuruma o tomete, michi o kiita hō ga ii yo.

⑥ **Does your place have Western-style beds?**

ベッドの部屋は、ありますか？

Beddo no heya wa, arimasu ka?

⑦ **There's nothing like the feel of the open road.**

広々した道をドライブするほど
気分のいいものは、ないね。

Hirobiroshita michi o doraibu suru hodo
kibun no ii mono wa, nai ne.

⑧ **Uh-oh, it looks like a massive traffic jam.**

おっと！　かなりひどい渋滞みたいだ……。

Otto! Kanari hidoi jūtai mitai da . . .

⑨ **Can we make a quick pit stop?**

ちょっと一休みしようか？

Chotto hitoyasumi shiyō ka?

## Lazing About

19_11

① **Sometimes it's nice to just do nothing.**

な〜んもしないっていうのも、たまにはいいね。

Nān mo shinai tte iu no mo, tamani wa ii ne.

② **We don't have any firm plans.**

とくに、これといった計画<sup></sup>もないんだ。

Tokuni kore to itta keikaku mo nai n' da.

③ **Let's have a picnic in the park.**

公園<sup></sup>でピクニックしようよ。

Kōen de pikunikku shiyō yo.

④ **I plan to sleep in all weekend.**

週末<sup></sup>は、寝<sup></sup>て過<sup></sup>ごすつもり。

Shūmatsu wa, nete sugosu tsumori.

⑤ **I'll be puttering around the house today.**

きょうは、うちでダラダラしてます。

Kyō wa, uchi de daradara shite 'masu.

## Reading and Watching TV

19_12

① **Did you see what was in the paper today?**

けさの新聞<sup></sup>、見<sup></sup>た？

Kesa no shimbun, mita?

② **I can't wake up without coffee and the paper.**

朝<sup></sup>は、コーヒーと新聞<sup></sup>がないと、

目<sup></sup>がさめないんです。

Asa wa, kōhī to shimbun ga nai to,

me ga samenai n' desu.

③ **That's a pretty risqué magazine!**
かなり、きわどい雑誌だね！
Kanari kiwadoi zasshi da ne!

④ **I'd like to subscribe, please.**
購読を申し込みたいんですけど。
Kōdoku o mōshikomitai n' desu kedo.

⑤ **You have got to read this!**
とにかく、これ、読んでみてよ！
Tonikaku, kore, yonde mite yo!

⑥ **I'm addicted to mystery novels.**
わたし、推理小説の中毒なんです。
Watashi, suiri-shōsetsu no chūdoku nan desu.

⑦ **I couldn't put the book down.**
読み出したら、やめられなくなっちゃった。
Yomidashitara, yamerarenakunatchatta.

⑧ **Anything good on TV tonight?**
今夜、何かおもしろいテレビ、やってるかな？
Kon'ya, nanika omoshiroi terebi, yatte 'ru ka na?

⑨ **Let's watch the soccer game tonight.**
今夜はテレビでサッカー見ようよ。
Kon'ya wa terebi de sakkā miyō yo.

⑩ **That show slays me!**
あの番組、めっちゃ、おもしろいよ！
Ano bangumi, metcha, omoshiroi yo!

Just for Fun

316

# Language Study

MP3
19_13

① **I want to speak better Japanese.**
もっと日本語が上手に話せるようになりたいです。
Motto Nihongo ga jōzu ni hanaseru yō ni naritai desu.

② **I can never remember how to say that.**
その言い回し、どうしても、おぼえられないんだ。
Sono iimawashi, dōshitemo oboerarenai n' da.

③ **Is there some way to say this in Japanese?**
これって、日本語でどう言ったらいいの？
Kore tte, Nihongo de dō ittara ii no?

④ **Say that again?**
もういちど、言ってくれる？
Mō ichido, itte kureru?

⑤ **I love this word!**
この言葉、いいねぇ！
Kono kotoba, ii nē!

⑥ **Saying that will land you in hot water.**
その言葉使うと、まずいことになるよ。
Sono kotoba tsukau to, mazui koto ni naru yo.

⑦ **My goal is to be able to read the newspapers.**
新聞が読めるようになるのが目標です。
Shimbun ga yomeru yōni naru no ga mokuhyō desu.

⑧ **I want to take private lessons.**
個人レッスン、受けたいな。
Kojin ressun, uketai na.

⑨ **You're an amazing teacher.**
先生の教え方は、すばらしいです！
Sensei no oshiekata wa, subarashii desu!

⑩ **I can speak Japanese, but I can't read it.**
日本語は話せるんだけど、
読むほうはダメなんです。
Nihongo wa hanaseru n' da kedo,
yomu hō wa dame nan desu.

⑪ **This phrasebook is the best!**
日本語をおぼえたいなら、この本だよね！
Nihongo o oboetai nara, kono hon da yo ne!

Just for Fun

## ACKNOWLEDGMENTS

When I think about whom I should thank for making this book possible, the endearing habit Japanese people have of complimenting any foreigner who makes a stab at speaking Japanese comes to mind. Japanese themselves make learning the language a rewarding and pleasant experience.

My initial introduction to Japan came through the amazing hospitality of my teachers and dear friends Midori Yajima and Shuichi Kato, and was funded through a Samuel T. Arnold Fellowship awarded by Brown University. I am undyingly grateful for the changes these brought to my life.

The actual production of this book was hugely improved by the invaluable input and suggestions from the following group of scholars, editors, and intellectuals: Yoko Kanda, Laura McCarthy, Mako Fukuda, Naruko Morisawa, Zeny Ocampos, Ed Turner, Kathy and David Muller, and members of the Nishimachi International School's Tomo no Kai. My deepest thanks to each of you.

I am also much indebted to the sparkling acting talents of Reiko Matsunaga and Tatsuhiro Nishinosono, and Katie Adler and Jeff Gedert, who vocalize the book's phrases in a clear and natural fashion, and to illustrator Shinsaku Sumi for adding subtle, succinct flair to these pages.

It is impossible to overstate the gratitude I have toward my editor, Kodansha International's talented Michael Staley, whose initial concept both Kyoko Tsuchiya and I found a delightful challenge to realize, and whose unflagging attention made this book rightfully as much his achievement as ours, and to my coauthor, translator Kyoko Tsuchiya, whose sense of humor, intelligence, and dedication made every phrase in this book a joy to discover. I would like to also thank Kodansha's Keiko Yoshida for her sharp editing skills and Kodansha International's Senior Editor Greg Starr for guidance.

Finally, I am hugely grateful for the words and support of my parents on both sides of the Pacific, Ichiko and Keinosuke Nagamura, and Hélène and Lester Pancoast; for the advice, assistance, and patience of my husband Mitsuhiro; and for some salient tips on current slang in both languages from my bilingual son, Léo. Kokoro kara, arigato gozaimasu!

Kit Pancoast Nagamura

**（英文版）会話のための日本語表現 1800**
The Ultimate Japanese Phrasebook
1800 Sentences for Everyday Use

2009 年 10 月 26 日　第 1 刷発行

| | |
|---|---|
| 著　者 | 長村キット |
| | 土屋京子 |
| 朗　読 | 松永玲子 |
| | 西ノ園達大 |
| | ケイティー・アドラー |
| | ジェフ・ゲダート |
| 挿　画 | 角 愼作 |
| 発行者 | 廣田浩二 |
| 発行所 | 講談社インターナショナル株式会社 |
| | 〒112-8652　東京都文京区音羽 1-17-14 |
| | 電話　03-3944-6493（編集部） |
| | 　　　03-3944-6492（営業部・業務部） |
| | ホームページ　www.kodansha-intl.com |
| 印刷・製本所 | 大日本印刷株式会社 |

落丁本、乱丁本は購入書店名を明記のうえ、講談社インターナショナル業務部宛
にお送りください。送料小社負担にてお取替えいたします。なお、この本につい
てのお問い合わせは、編集部宛にお願いいたします。本書の無断複写（コピー）
は著作権法上での例外を除き、禁じられています。

定価はカバーに表示してあります。